The

Board

Manual

Frederick H. Bair, Jr.

Planners Press

American Planning Association
Washington, D.C.
Chicago, Illinois

*Dedicated to the many who serve faithfully and well
on zoning boards and often get little thanks for it.
You have ours.*

Copyright 1984 by the American Planning Association
1313 E. 60th St., Chicago, IL 60637

ISBN 918286-32-8
Library of Congress Catalog Card Number 84-060300
Printed in the United States of America

Contents

Foreword

The zoning board—in some places called the board of appeals, and in others the board of adjustment—has played an important role in zoning administration for about three quarters of a century. There are several thousand zoning boards in the United States, and tens of thousands of zoning board members. From the start, these board members have generally been citizens without any technical background in planning or in zoning.

And while zoning boards have been around for about 75 years, citizens serving on zoning boards have had few published sources to which they could turn for help. From time to time, state or regional agencies would publish short brochures or pamplets that never really covered the complexity of the job. Thus, the APA Planners Press is quite pleased to publish the first national manual for zoning boards.

Professionals and lay people familiar with Fred's previous writing know that he writes with clarity and attention to technical detail. In this book he has, of course, done it again.

Frank S. So
Deputy Executive Director
American Planning Association

Introduction

The zoning board of adjustment or appeals has important duties. Its functions, partly administrative and partly judicial, are defined and limited by state enabling legislation and by provisions of local zoning adopted under such acts.

Boards of this kind existed before 1920 and generally stem from a common ancestor, the New York City Board of Appeals. Today their powers, duties, and procedures usually follow those set forth in the *Standard State Zoning Enabling Act*, published by the U.S. Department of Commerce in the mid–1920s. Standard Act provisions concerning boards of adjustment were in effect verbatim in 40 states in 1972, and were used with relatively minor variations in most of the others, according to Norman Williams, Jr., in *American Land Planning Law.*[1]

The Standard Act relied heavily on state-enacted charter amendments for New York City and portions of the New York City *Building Zone Resolution*, although there were some changes in provisions concerning the size and qualifications of members of boards of adjustment, and in terminology referring to actions of such boards.

Similarity in enabling act language concerning boards, and in actions of such boards, gives rise to a supplementary source of general guidance. Courts have interpreted the language and reviewed a large number of board actions (considerably more than should have been necessary had boards operated within their limits and used prescribed procedures). Although consensus among state courts is by no means complete, it is near enough so that on many issues there are now helpful guidelines on findings boards should make before rendering decisions and on procedures to follow.

This book is divided into five chapters. A few comments about organization and contents seem appropriate:

Chapter 1, *Historical Orientation*, traces the roots of the zoning board concept. Many zoning concepts have evolved over the years. The degree to which the modern board is based on early ordinances and models is amazing—even the mistakes and confusion seem to have come down intact.

Chapter 2, *The Powers of the Board and Limitations on Their Use*, discusses various types of zoning board actions and procedures. Duties include (and are usually limited to) actions on appeals from decisions of administrative officials, special exceptions, and variances. The distinctions between special exceptions and variances are made clear. Ordinance language on special exceptions and guidelines for variances are provided.

Chapter 3, *Exercises in the Application of Principles Concerning Variances*, discusses common types of cases that come before zoning boards. These include, for example, substandard lots of record, nonconforming lots of record, reduction of required off-street parking and the reduction of lots and yards.

Chapter 4, *Rules of the Board: Models, with Commentary*, details guides (including those in state legislation and local ordinances) for conduct of the board business. This comprehensive chapter is the longest in the book. Good rules, if clearly written, understood, and followed, are the foundation of good board performance. Topics cover membership, meetings, offices, records, appeals, public notice, staff, duties of the zoning administrator, conduct of the board and staff members, procedures at hearings, executive sessions, records, and rehearings.

Chapter 5, *Improved Current Zoning Practice*, addresses persistent problems and offers suggestions for improvements. In particular, there is a hierarchy of special permits that could help sort out types of cases and promote improvement and expedition of administration.

No manual intended for general use by boards in this country can reflect all the variations in current state enabling legislation, decisions of state courts on similar issues, or provisions of local ordinances assigning duties and indicating how they should be performed. Users of this manual should also be guided by five other principal references:

1. Their own state zoning enabling legislation.

2. Court determinations in their state. Generally these will have been analyzed in guides prepared by state agencies or universities, or in articles in law journals. Counsel to the board may have detailed case reports.

3. The comprehensive plan, which zoning is intended to follow.

4. The rules of the board itself.

Boards exercising only those powers assigned to them by law, and exercising them in the manner provided by law, perform their intended public function of protecting the public interest. They may disappoint those affected by their decisions, but boards winning for their friends at the expense of the public interest add to judicial case loads. Even-handed justice is not always popular, but it is essential to effective zoning.

Note

1. Norman Williams, Jr., *American Land Planning Law: Land Use and the Police Power* (Chicago: Callaghan and Co., 1974), Vol. 1, §18.08.

1
Historical Orientation

Evolution of Building and Land-Use Regulations in the United States

Early American building and land-use controls grew from disasters. Gunpowder mills were required to locate on the outskirts of town, to the occasional inconvenience of owners and workers. Major conflagrations led to controls on construction materials. Boston, in 1692, required new buildings to be stone or brick, with slate or tile roofs:

> unless in particular Cases where Necessity requires, being so judged and signified in Writing under the Hands of the Justices and Selectmen of said Town, or major part of both; the Governour with the Advice and Consent of the Council, shall see cause to grant Licenses unto any person to build with Timber, or to cover with Shingle.[1]

Here was both regulation and provision for rare variance. From such origins came our current fire zone requirements.

Big-city housing congestion and squalor led to enactment of tenement laws around 1900, as predecessors to present housing codes. Building codes set minimum construction standards. Sanitary codes were an answer to health hazards. Height ordinances were adopted to facilitate fire protection, keep streets from becoming dark canyons, and reduce fire death tolls. Nuisance ordinances covered a variety of problem areas.

There is a pattern in the way such controls originate, are adopted, and spread. Society grows in mass and complexity. Frictions and disasters proliferate, and with them regulations—on land use, on construction, on occupancy of buildings and land. Public awareness, alarm, indignation about a problem, reach the point where it is politically expedient— sometimes politically mandatory—to adopt regulations. The regulations are opposed by those who make them necessary, joined by opponents of *any* further extension of government into private affairs.

Once established, new forms of control are often challenged in the courts. The judiciary, properly conservative on property and personal rights, first rejects the innovations, and then, on demonstration of real and pressing public need, accepts them, with warnings as to how far extension of such controls will be tolerated.

After the example is set, other jurisdictions imitate it, often without adequate understanding of reasons either for substantive requirements or procedural rituals.

(As qualifying comments on these broad generalizations: Original efforts on parallel lines may start in several jurisdictions at about the same time.

There is often crusading zeal about the new control and its marvelous curative properties, and strong missionary efforts to encourage widespread imitation. This is only partly because of conviction of merit. There is also the feeling that breadth of application signifies assurance of virtue, lessening probability of judicial opposition. "If it is common, it must be right."

Those who regulate, and courts judging regulation, become more tolerant as urban pressures grow and particular regulatory forms entrench themselves. The scope of original controls enlarges. Substantive requirements and limitations increase.)

The New York City Zoning Model and Its Influences

Zoning is an example of how the pattern operates. What happened in New York City before 1920 explains much of what is happening in zoning all over the country today.

From 1914–16, the New York State legislature granted amendments to the *Greater New York Charter*, allowing the city to be divided into districts (or zones—hence the term zoning) and within each district to regulate and restrict uses, height, bulk, and location of buildings, and the area of yards, courts, and other open spaces. As a novel feature (for the time), such regulations could vary from one district to another, but must apply uniformly within each district.

In 1916, under this new authority, the first *New York City Building Zone Resolution* was adopted, after six years of preparation. Supporters of this untried form of regulation worried about its survival and pushed for its application in as many other jurisdictions as possible. Edward M.

Bassett, a prime mover for zoning and a principal author of both the *Charter* amendments and the zoning resolution, explained why in the preface to his classic *Zoning*,[2] which provides background material for much of what follows here.

> After the zoning plan was adopted by New York City, a citizens' committee, called the Zoning Committee of New York, was established to assist in the administration of the new law in New York City, and to help extend zoning throughout the country. It was feared that if this rather new innovation of the police power was employed in only one city, courts would frown on it because of its limited use. The future of zoning was at that time precarious and it was considered that its extension to other cities would be an aid to securing the approval of the courts. Judicial approval of extensions of the police power depends somewhat on a widespread opinion that such extensions are needed, and also upon their actual employment by governing bodies.

Other cities were slow to follow New York's example until the zoning resolution was upheld by New York State's highest court in 1920. Even after that, state judicial response was not uniformly favorable. In Ohio, a U.S. District Court declared emphatically in *Euclid v. Ambler* not only that zoning as applied to the land in question was unreasonable, but that the Euclid ordinance as a whole was fundamentally and basically illegal and unsupportable, offending both the U.S. and Ohio constitutions. The U.S. Supreme Court reversed this decision in 1926, declaring, in effect, that *reasonable zoning is constitutional.*

(Board members may not be long in office before they are assured by agitated but uninformed persons that zoning is patently unconstitutional and part of an insidious plot, communistic in effect if not origin, designed to undermine the American Way of Life. The U.S. Supreme Court settled the matter of constitutionality long ago. Whether zoning is reasonable depends, among other things, on its substantial relation to public purpose, a matter to be tested on a case-by-case basis. As to left-wing influence, neither Secretary of Commerce Herbert Hoover nor the members of the Advisory Committee leaned excessively in this direction.)

The Advisory Committee on Zoning and the Standard State Zoning Enabling Act

In the early twenties, Secretary of Commerce Herbert Hoover appointed the Advisory Committee on Zoning. This prestigious group, conservative in both sponsorship and makeup, depended heavily on New York experience in preparing the Standard State Zoning Enabling Act, although it made some modifications to facilitate application in a variety of jurisdictions. Section 7 of the Standard Act, *Boards of Adjustments*, contains a number of such changes, not always for the better. As it appears in the 1926 version, still the basis of zoning in most states, Section 7 includes over half the language of the entire act, indicating major concern with this body and its functions.

In the light of later experience with such boards, the concern was well founded.

At least part of the problems which arose may be charged against the Advisory Committee. Its members were eminently qualified in their own fields (lawyers, realtors, engineers, housing consultants, and landscape architects representing major national organizations), but none of them was an editor. The turgid prose and conglomerate nature of Section 7 makes it a difficult guide.

Division of Functions: The New York City Model

In New York's pioneering effort, the framework for division of powers and performance of functions, established by charter amendments passed by the state legislature, was as follows:

The Commission on Building Districts and Restrictions, an appointed advisory body, prepared recommendations as to *original* district boundaries and regulations, made a tentative report, and held public hearings. It then submitted its final report to

The Board of Estimate and Apportionment, a body composed of the mayor, the controller, the president of the board of aldermen, and five borough presidents, all elected officials. The charter amendments empowered this board to adopt zoning regulations, but only after receiving the final report and after holding a further public hearing. This board was also empowered to amend the regulations after public notice and hearing, but the Commission on Building Districts and Restrictions was not involved in preparing or processing amendments.

The Board of Standards and Appeals, taken as a whole, consisted of the fire commissioner, the chief of the uniformed fire department, the superintendent of buildings, and six other members appointed by the mayor. This group was largely concerned with making a broad range of administrative rules and regulations, including construction, fire, and labor codes. When operating as a whole, it had no appellate functions.

These were reserved to

The Board of Appeals, a subgroup made up of the six appointed members (one of whom was chairman of both boards) and the chief of the fire department. Appeal from decisions of this body was to the courts.

Original appointments were for overlapping terms, succeeding appointments for three years. No member of the board was allowed to pass upon any question in which he or any corporation in which he was a stockholder or security holder, or had an interest. Strong professional and technical qualifications were specifically required for four of the six appointed members:

The chairman, designated as such by the mayor, was required to be an architect or structural engineer with at least fifteen years experience. While serving, he was prohibited from engaging in any other occupation. One each of the remaining members was required to have at least ten years experience as an architect, a builder, or a structural engineer. All members were well compensated.

In retrospect, the organizational arrangement appears to have been an enviable device for coordinating rule-making and appellate procedures in related fields. The present fragmented approach seems considerably less intelligent.

Division of Functions: The Standard Act Adaptation

Adaptation of the New York model for zoning application only, and for general use as a standard state zoning enabling act affecting both large and small jurisdictions, presented a number of problems. Some of the solutions leave much to be desired.

The Zoning Commission. When the Standard Act was drafted, planning commissions were relatively scarce. The Standard Act, at Section 6, required appointment of an advisory body, the zoning commission. The zoning commission was to recommend boundaries of original districts and regulations to apply therein, make a preliminary report and hold public hearings on it. The legislative body could not hold its hearings or take action until it had received the final report of the zoning commission. (The zoning commission was *not* the board of adjustment— see below.)

Like its progenitor, the Commission on Building Districts and Restrictions, the zoning commission was an ad hoc group expiring after its final report had been submitted. It did not deal with proposed amendments.

This was unfortunate and would have been more so except for the provision in Section 6 that, where a planning commission existed, it might be appointed as the zoning commission. With the passage of time, many states have changed Standard Act language to give the planning commission prime responsibility both for preparation of the original ordinance and for processing amendments prior to legislative action.

The Legislative Body. Under Standard Act terms, the function of the legislative body is parallel in zoning matters to that performed by the Board of Estimate and Apportionment in New York City. It is the only body empowered to adopt or amend the ordinance. This reservation of legislative control has been an important turning point in many cases where boards of adjustment have exceeded their powers and taken actions amounting to changes in zoning.

Absence of General Coordinating Board on Construction, Fire, Occupancy, and Zoning. Nothing equivalent to the Board of Standards and Appeals was carried forward to Standard Act language. Preoccupation at the time was with zoning, the new regulatory device, rather than on continued evolution of a coordinated control system. With affected jurisdictions varying widely as to size, governmental organization, and kinds of regulation in effect, a general prescription for a similar board might have been difficult to develop, but some alternative courses might have been arranged.

The Board of Adjustment. Although the Board of Standards and Appeals has no counterpart under the Standard Act, its "subcommittee" Board of Appeals was carried forward as the board of adjustment (now appearing under several variations in title). Provisions concerning membership on the board appear early in Section 7:

> Section 7. Board of Adjustment — Such local legislative body may provide for the appointment of a board of adjustment. . . .The board of adjustment shall consist of five members, each to be appointed for a term of three years and removable for cause by the appointing authority upon written charges and after public hearing. Vacancies shall be filled for the unexpired term of any member whose term becomes vacant.

This adaptation leaves much to be desired on several counts. There is no provision for overlapping terms, which would often leave the board without continuity of experience (except that many jurisdictions went ahead and overlapped terms anyway, or appointed members to succeed themselves). There is no prohibition of action in cases where board members have conflicts of interest—a grave omission, considering the record of some boards. And no qualifications whatever are set for board members.

Under the New York arrangement, a well-qualified, well-paid board with a full-time chairman was responsible to a considerable extent for drafting and adopting a broad range of administrative rules and regulations. Its appellate subcommittee was responsible (a) for interpretation of such controls on appeal from decisions of administrative officials; (b) for making determinations and decisions in specified use exception cases under the zoning resolution; and (c) for varying strict application of the letter of the law in cases of practical difficulties or unnecessary hardships involving zoning or any of the other controls within its jurisdiction.

Under the Standard Act, a board (usually uncompensated), whose members usually had nothing to do with framing original controls, which has no powers to adopt or amend either legislative enactments or administrative regulations, and which has no required qualifications for members, is expected to perform parallel functions, but only in relation to zoning. (In most jurisdictions, one or several other boards, usually with specified qualifications for members, go their separate ways in performing appellate and administrative duties in connection with construction, housing, health and fire codes.)

In the absence of qualification requirements, many boards have been dominated by members representing special interests and desiring to manipulate zoning for their own ends, or members whose interests or sympathies run counter to sound zoning. Occasionally boards are composed of members who feel the urge to correct what they believe to be errors in zoning regulations and refuse to be limited in their actions to functions assigned and limited by law.

Bassett observes: "A board of appeals is presumed to be composed of experts."[3] Presumption does not create expertise.

These are among reasons why it has long been said that boards of adjustment, created as safety valves for zoning, have become the leak in the boiler, impairing zoning's effectiveness rather than contributing to its efficient and equitable operation.

Some Early (and Continuing) Problems with Boards of Adjustment

In many jurisdictions, theory and practice on boards of adjustment parted early. Too often, the breach is still apparent.

In 1927, E. T. Hartman, Executive Secretary of the Massachusetts Federation of Planning Boards, wrote in *The American City:*

I think that the most critical point in regard to the whole zoning scheme lies in board of appeals administration, where a board assumes the power to vary the law to suit itself, and where, as is now happening, personal interest, favoritism, politics and cash affect the opinions of members of boards of appeals, no law will produce satisfactory results.[4]

The city that was the model for the Standard Enabling Act became a prime example of abuses by its board. By 1927, according to Seymour Toll, the Citizens' Union, a New York City reform group, was demanding a purge of the graft-ridden Board of Appeals, and in 1931 a special state legislative committee began the famous Seabury investigations into board corruption:

If all that had happened was the corruption of public office, it would have been historically monotonous business. American municipal villainy did not have to wait upon zoning to find its first expression. The original feature of this particular bit of malfeasance was its imposition upon what was supposed to be an initial and important effort to make a planning device into an American legal institution. Both business and political decision-makers in a great American city were profoundly indifferent to even the most modest efforts at using law to help the city grow intelligently.

The twenties were years which not only produced zoning in hundreds of American cities but also a standard technique for subverting its administration.[5]

At short range, quality of regulations is an academic question if the board ignores them. Too many boards, intended to serve the public by applying "discretion of experts to exceptional circumstances," willfully or negligently disregard clearly established requirements as to procedures and findings and substitute capricious indiscretions of amateurs in any circumstances they happen to choose. Malfeasance is destructive to public confidence in zoning, and to the fabric of zoning, whether grounded in well-meaning or in venal motives.

At longer range, good regulations are helpful to the courts in reversing wrongful actions, but the board, in such cases, becomes an impediment in the road to justice rather than a means for providing it.

Some Problems with Language and How They Originated

A new discipline tends to develop new language, or to warp established meanings to its own ends. Zoning has been doing so since its beginnings.

(The process is not completed. Now that the basic terms are reasonably well understood by regulators, regulatees and the courts, the American Law Institute's *Model Land Development Code,* part of which covers the same ground as the Standard Act, changes terminology. Thus in states adopting the *Code,* the process of public education and judicial interpetation must start over.) Early zoning and zoning enabling legislation was clearly put together by committees whose members had diverse opinions as to what various terms should be, meant, or should mean. On matters relating to the board of adjustment, doubts as to how far zoning could or should go are reflected in verbiage leaving plenty of room for maneuver.

Uncertainty as to the meaning of words and phrases created problems for early boards and for the courts. The area of uncertainty has diminished with judicial interpretation and with closer, but still evolving, definition of what zoning may or may not do. Courts are now considerably more liberal in their interpretations than at the beginning, but have their limits.

Two terms of art evolved early, *variance* and *special exception.* These will be discussed in context later, but their early history accounts for continuing difficulties. Neither term appeared as such in the New York charter or zoning resolution, but the seeds of both were there.

The charter, at Section 719-5, gave the Board of Appeals power to "vary or modify" any rule or regulation, or the provisions of any existing law or ordinance relating to construction or structural alteration (but not use) on grounds of practical difficulty or unnecessary hardship. Insofar as practicable, such decisions were to be "in the form of a general statement or resolution which shall be applicable to cases similar to or falling within the principles passed upon in such decision." Here, because of the generality rule, there was no provision for conditions and safeguards to apply in particular cases.

The zoning resolution, at Section 7, *Use District Exceptions,* assigned the board the duty to "determine and vary the application of the use district regulations" in specific listed cases, and to apply appropriate conditions and safeguards. The generality rule did not apply here, because individual cases were involved, such as lots divided by use district boundaries, telephone exchanges in residential districts, or temporary and conditional uses and structures in undeveloped sections.

As the Standard Act emerged from the Advisory Committee, to "vary and modify" on grounds of hardship was termed "variance." To "determine and vary" in cases specifically identified in the ordinance, and without the element of hardship, was classed as "special exception." The distinction was useful, although it was blurred by injudicious use of scissors and pastepot in constructing Section 7 of the Standard Act.

The problem arises because at the beginning of Section 7, and only there, "special exception" is apparently used as a generic term, to include both specific special exceptions and variances. The initial paragraph, authorizing creation of the board, states that the local legislative body:

> may provide that the said board of adjustment may, in appropriate cases and subject to appropriate conditions and safeguards, make special exceptions to the terms of the ordinance in harmony with its general purpose and intent and in accordance with general or specific rules therein contained.

This is the only statement concerning powers of the board at this point. Section 7 then proceeds for six paragraphs on other matters, and in the seventh provides a detailed listing of powers:

1. To hear and decide appeals where it is alleged there is error in any order, requirement, decision, or determination made by a administrative official in the enforcement of this act or of any ordinance adopted pursuant thereto.

2. To hear and decide special exceptions to the terms of the ordinance upon which such board is required to pass under such ordinance.

3. To authorize upon appeal in specific cases such variance from the terms of the ordinance as will not be contrary to the public interest, where, owing to special conditions, a literal enforcement of the provisions of the ordinance will result in unnecessary hardship, and so that the spirit of the ordinance shall be observed and substantial justice done.

Had the initial entry concerning powers been omitted and the detailed listing appropriately amended, the following matters would have been clarified:

a. Conditions and safeguards may be attached in connection with *either* special exceptions or variances, and not merely with special exceptions alone (as strict interpretation would indicate). Bassett, dean of early zoners, makes it clear that the broader application was intended: "Conditions may be imposed on a variance permit."[6]

b. General or specific rules may be included in the ordinance concerning *either* variances or special exceptions, and not merely the latter.

Partly as a result of this editorial ineptitude, boards of adjustment and the courts were long confused about the distinction between the variance and the special exception. Some still are.

As late as 1951, the Florida Supreme Court, in *Troup v. Bird*, 53 So.2d, 717, opined:

> The granting of a variance or exception usually contemplates only a special exception to existing zoning rules . . . in a special instance permitting a nonconforming use in order to alleviate undue burden or unnecessary hardship upon the property owner. . . .

The permit that the Supreme Court upheld in its opinion confusing variances and special exceptions was neither, nor does either permit a nonconforming use, as the term is generally defined.

Notes

1. James Metzenbaum, *Law of Zoning* (Mt. Kisco, N.Y.: Baker, Voorhis & Co., 1955), Vol. 1, p. 4.

2. Edward M. Bassett, *The Laws, Administration, and Court Decisions During the First Twenty Years* (New York: Russell Sage Foundation, 1970), pp. 7–8 (hereafter cited as Bassett's *Zoning*).

3. Bassett's *Zoning*, p. 128.

4. "Zoning's Greatest Danger—Lawless Acts by Boards of Appeals," in *The American City*, August 1927, pp. 231–4.

5. Seymour I. Toll, *Zoned America* (New York: Grossman Publishers, 1969), pp. 209–10.

6. Bassett's *Zoning*, p. 128.

2
The Powers of the Board and Limitations on Their Use

We recently ran across another board of adjustment being richly generous with other people's zoning. It happens from time to time. This one was rezoning (via use variances) for commerce along a residential street because the city commission had made a mistake, the board chairman said.

We like most of the people we have met on boards of adjustment. We even liked this man—he didn't know what he was doing or what he was supposed to be doing, but he had a wonderful spirit about it, and the members of his board were right in there pitching with him, strewing commerce up and down streets, distributing zoning largesse to distressed widows and orphans, and being generally helpful. He dwelt at some length on the good he and his board had been able to do through the years they had worked together.

The town is now past zoning remedy. Gas stations festoon the most unlikely corners with their gay flags and friendly, beckoning signs. They snuggle against staid old residences rejuvenating, under their influence, with plastic fronts, beauty parlors, TV repair shops, undertaking establishments (and multitudinous For Rent notices). Billboards gladden the eye wherever there was a happy combination of location, destitution, and an enterprising operator. Everywhere there is a comfortable informality bordering (at least) on disorder.[1]

The case load of the board is light if the ordinance is good, heavy if it is bad, and increases rapidly if it becomes apparent that the board is easily manipulated. Entirely too many zoning ordinances are poorly written, badly organized and indefinite on matters relating to the board. Where board performance is substandard the blame can as often be laid to defective guidelines as to the fact that the board ignores the guidelines established.

Standard Act provisions give the board three powers. The quotation above indicates the result of abuse. Because such abuse has been widespread, courts have laid down rules. State enabling legislation should reflect these, to make them apply generally. But many improvements can be made locally, without waiting for state action, so long as the local changes do not conflict with the state law.

To indicate how a modern ordinance reflects such provisions, Standard Act language is contrasted below with provisions of the proposed Atlanta, Georgia, zoning ordinance. As cited below, Standard Act provisions have been reorganized to remedy editorial deficiencies in its original form, but no substantive changes have been made.

Appeals from Decisions of Administrative Officials

Standard Act, Section 7

The board of adjustment shall have the following powers:

1. To hear and decide appeals where it is alleged there is error in any order, requirement, decision, or determination made by an administrative official in the enforcement of this act or of any ordinance adopted pursuant thereto.

Appeals to the board of adjustment may be taken by any person aggrieved or by any officer, department, board or bureau of the municipality affected by any decision of the administrative officer. Such appeal shall be taken within a reasonable time, as provided by the rules of the board, by filing with the officer from whom the appeal is taken and with the board of adjustment a notice of appeal specifying the grounds thereof . . . .

Proposed Atlanta Ordinance

1308. *Specific Powers, Duties and Functions; Limitations.*

The Board shall have the following powers and duties:

1308.1. *Appeals from Decisions of Administrative Official.*

To hear and decide appeals where it is alleged there is error in any order, requirement, decision or determination of an administrative official (to be construed as including any department, bureau, board or commission) in the administration and enforcement of this ordinance. Such appeals may be taken by any person aggrieved or by any officer, department, board or bureau affected by any decision of the administrative official from whom the appeal is taken and with the Board, a notice of appeal specifying the grounds thereof, *within 30 days* after the action appealed from was taken,

An appeal stays all proceedings in furtherance of the action appealed from, unless the officer from whom the appeal is taken certifies to the board of adjustment after the notice of appeal shall have been filed with him that by reason of facts stated in the certificate a stay would, in his opinion, cause imminent peril to life or property. In such case, proceedings shall not be stayed otherwise than by a restraining order which may be granted by the board of adjustment or by a court of record on application, on notice to the officer from whom the appeal is taken and on due cause shown.

The board of adjustment shall fix a reasonable time for the hearing of the appeal, give public notice thereof, as well as due notice to the parties in interest, and decide the same within a reasonable time. Upon the hearing, any party may appear in person or by agent or by attorney.

unless the rules of the board specify a longer period generally or for particular classes of cases.

An appeal stays all legal proceedings in furtherance of the action appealed from, unless the official from whom the appeal is taken certifies to the board, after notice of appeal shall have been filed with him, that by reason of facts stated in the certificate a stay would, in his opinion, cause imminent peril to life and property. In such a case, proceedings shall not be stayed otherwise than by a restraining order which may be granted by the board of adjustment or a court of record on application, on notice to the officer from whom the appeal is taken, and on due cause shown.

The Board shall fix a reasonable time for the hearing of the appeal and given public notice thereof as well as due notice to the parties in interest. Upon the hearing, any party may appeal in person or by agent or by attorney.

The Board shall decide the appeal within a reasonable time.

An appeal shall be sustained only if the Board finds that the administrative official's action was based on an erroneous finding of a material fact, or that he acted in an arbitrary or capricious manner or manifestly abused his discretion.

In exercising the above-mentioned powers such board may, in conformity with the provisions of this act, reverse or affirm, wholly or partly, or may modify the order, requirement, decision or determination appealed from and may make such order, requirement, decision, or determination as ought to be made, and to that end shall have all the powers of the officer from whom the appeal is taken.

In exercising its powers, the board may reverse or affirm, wholly or partly, or may modify the order, requirement, decision or determination appealed from, and to that end shall have all the powers of the administrative official from whom the appeal was taken and may issue or direct the issuance of a permit.
(Italicized text above is added matter.)

Board actions in this class of cases generally constitute only a minor part of their workload, particularly where the ordinance is well and clearly drawn and officials are competent.

Language is added to basic Standard Act terms in the proposed Atlanta ordinance, allowing reversal of the decision of an administrative official only upon findings that he erred on material facts, which would include misinterpretation of the ordinance, or acted in an arbitrary or capricious manner or manifestly abused his discretion. This addition is intended to reduce any tendency of the board to engage in legislative activity beyond its powers in "correcting" what it may consider to be errors in the ordinance. The example below may clarify the distinction.

An Example: Appeal from Decision of Administrative Official
The administrative official should act only in strict accord with the terms of the ordinance. He discovers by complaint of neighbors that a babysitting service has been established in a neighborhood in which child care centers (not adequately defined) require a special exception. No special exception has been obtained. He calls the violation to the attention of the alleged offenders and orders them to cease operations.

The appeal to the board alleges that a mere baby-sitting service, conducted occasionally and in their own home and seldom with more than four children involved, is different from a child care center. It does not require licensing from the State Board of Health, as does a child care center, and should be considered a mere home occupation, customary and incidental in residential surroundings. Grandparents in the vicinity do the same sort of thing (although not for pay), and the effect on the neighborhood is the same.

Without going into all possible permutations of decisions in this case, one which is valid and one which is not are suggested below.

The board may find that baby-sitting in the home of the operators is indeed a customary home occupation, even though a fee is charged, noting that its operational characteristics, rather than whether or not it is commercial, should distinguish it from a child care center, and that if a baby-sitter went to the home of clients there would be no question about the matter even though the same number of children were involved. Hence the ruling of the administrative official is in error, and is reversed. No special exception is required, and the operation may continue. This decision would be proper, in terms of the role of the board.

On the other hand, the board may find that baby-sitting in the home of the operators is in the same class with operation of a child care center, noting that some child care centers have four or less children on occasion and charge a fee. In its determination in this case, however, the board gives considerable weight to the fact that the State Board of Health regulates child care centers, and overlapping control by the zoning ordinance seems undesirable. It reverses the decision of the administrator on such grounds, indicating that he should not harass the appellants further. Here the board has overstepped its jurisdictional boundaries. (Part of the problem often lies in loose definitions in the ordinance.)

Similarly, the board should not be influenced in its decisions by its opinions as to whether the ordinance or specific provisions are unconstitutional, or were validly enacted.

A Note on Stay of Proceedings

"Stay of proceedings" language cited above deserves special comment and analysis. Taking the immediately preceding example, the action appealed from was that of the administrative official in requiring that the baby-sitting operation be stopped, as a violation of the ordinance. On filing of the appeal, "all proceedings in furtherance of the action appealed from" are stayed—in other words, the operation may continue until the board settles the matter (or the courts make a determination on appeal from the board's decision).

An exception is provided for this rule, in cases where there is imminent peril to life and property. In the case of the baby-sitting service, the administrative official might certify to the board (or a court) that the residence is an old, highly flammable frame building, with obsolete wiring inadequate for the electric room heaters being used. It is a firetrap, and he states his belief that a stay would cause imminent peril. On grounds like these, the board (or court) might order the baby-sitting operation discontinued before a decision on the appeal.

Although Standard Act language on stay of proceedings is so located as to appear to apply generally to appeals from decisions of administrative officials and to appeals for variances (and to applications for special exceptions only if "appeal" is construed to include "application," which stretches the language inordinately), in actual practice it would apply almost exclusively only to the first variety—the appeal from the administrative official's decision. Another variant of the baby-sitter case might be helpful:

If the board decided that a child care center special exception was indeed required (upholding the original position of the administrative official) and the appellants forthwith applied for the special exception, would the stay apply?

It should not. In the first place, strict interpretation of the language of the ordinance (and of enabling legislation) does not allow for a stay in the case of applications for special exceptions. Second, the board has now concurred that a violation exists. Good enforcement requires that violations should cease. The mere fact that the party apprehended now begins proceedings to seek a special exception should not justify allowing the violation to continue.

Special Exceptions

Concerning special exceptions, Standard Act language is brief, general, and lacks any standards whatever. As indicated earlier, the initial reference to special exceptions at the beginning of Section 7 apparently used the term in a generic sense to cover both special exceptions and variances. The board may, "in appropriate cases and subject to appropriate conditions and safeguards, make special exceptions to the terms of the ordinance in harmony with its general purpose and intent and in accordance with general or specific rules therein contained."

In the detailed listing of powers of the board which appears several paragraphs further on, the second reads: "To hear and decide special exceptions to the terms of the ordinance upon which such board is required to pass under such ordinance."

No appeal is involved in special exceptions. This is an area of original jurisdiction for the board, and it is here acting in an administrative rather than quasi-judicial capacity.

In special exception cases, the determination to be made is whether the proposal meets the purposes and requirements of the ordinance concerning the particular use. The board may not originate its own special exceptions. It can act only on those specifically assigned for its attention.

Those who draft regulations should be careful to make it clear that any action required of the board other than in the case of appeals from administrative decisions or variances is a special exception, since the three powers are all the board has. Thus many ordinances have provisions authorizing the board, in cases where a zoning boundary splits a lot, to permit an extension of the regulations for either portion of the lot not to exceed a specified distance into the remaining portion. So stated, it is not clear under what power the board is operating, or what procedures should apply. To clarify matters, the entry should begin: "Where a zoning boundary splits a lot, the board of adjustment may, *as a special exception*, permit the extension . . . ." (Emphasis supplied.)

Distinctions Between Special Exceptions and Variances
The special exception is permissible if the application meets the requirements set forth in the ordinance. The variance involves relaxation of the rules of the ordinance, within limits established.

The special exception does not involve the element of unnecessary hardship. Grant of a variance should be grounded in a demonstration of such hardship.

Special exceptions are specifically set forth in the ordinance and may be applied in many locations within districts in which they are permissible. Specific variances are not set forth in the ordinance and apply only to individual properties.

Special exceptions generally concern uses. Variances generally should not.

Ordinance Provisions Concerning Special Exceptions
A great deal should be done in local controls to flesh out the incomplete skeleton of Standard Act language. Things which need doing include the following:

Statements of Intent. There should be a general statement of intent defining special exceptions and indicating why they are necessary and the circumstances under which they are to be granted. In addition, on many classes of special exceptions or individual exception items, it will be helpful to the board (and the courts, if it comes to that) to provide intent statements in the ordinance. There is a general rule that regulations must have a substantial relation to public purpose. The intent statement establishes that purpose, guides in determinations as to appropriate location, and provides a basis for requiring conditions and safeguards.

Procedural Information.   The ordinance should indicate where applications for special exceptions are to be filed; the form of the application; the manner in which hearings are to be scheduled; and the manner of publication of notice. There should be indication as to a time limit for board actions.

Findings Required, Generally, and on Specific Items.   As a checklist for the board and to assure the preparation of a complete record in case of court review, the ordinance should establish requirements as to specific findings to be made before a special exception is granted. This may be done in two stages, one applying to special exceptions generally (reducing the need for repetitive language), and the other involving additional criteria applying to subclasses of special exceptions or individual special exception items. The ordinance should also require the board to state specific reasons in case of denial of application.

Conditions and Safeguards.   The ordinance might well indicate generally that conditions and safeguards may be attached to special exceptions as necessary to protect the public interest (with identification of the public interest being protected required as a deterrent to arbitrary or capricious conditions). Again, there may be a two-stage statement, with increased particularity in connection with subclasses of special exceptions or individual items.

The ordinance might also authorize requirement of a guarantee or bond for maintenance of required safeguards. Either in the general section on violations or in this section, there should be an indication that violation of conditions or safeguards is to be construed as violation of the ordinance.

Special Exceptions Apply to Property, Not Person.   Special exceptions generally apply to the property involved, not to the person. Concern of the board is with what is to be done and how, rather than with who is to do it. Regulations are intended to be applied equally to each class and kind of buildings within a district, and introducing the personal element would remove this equitable treatment. The ordinance should make note of this.

Withdrawal of Applications; Rehearing if Withdrawn or Denied.   Boards usually have enough to do without frequently repeated hearings of the same cases. Applicants appearing at hearings and sensing extensive opposition in the audience have been known to attempt to wear it down by withdrawals after the hearing begins. For both of these reasons, it is desirable to establish in the ordinance a time period after denial or withdrawal before substantially the same special exception may be considered. (Similar provisions often cover appeals for variances and amendment requests.)

Atlanta Proposed Ordinance Provisions Illustrating Points Made
Provisions from the proposed Atlanta ordinance as cited below illustrate application of these principles:

1308.2. *Special Exceptions.*

The board shall have the power to hear and decide applications for such special exceptions as may be specifically authorized by this ordinance, in accordance with requirements set forth herein.

1308.2.2. *Intent Concerning Special Exceptions.*

Within the city generally, or within certain zoning districts, certain uses specified in this ordinance are of a nature requiring special and intensive review to determine whether they should be permitted in specified locations, and the special conditions and safeguards which should be applied if permission is granted in such locations. Special exception procedures as provided herein are intended to assure that such review is made and that appropriate conditions and safeguards are attached. Special exception procedures shall be applied, and special exceptions granted, only as, and in cases, specified in this ordinance.

1308.2.2. *Applications for Special Exceptions.*

Applications for special exceptions shall be filed with the administrative official, on forms and with supporting material as required by the rules of the board. The administrative official shall establish an agenda for public hearing, cause notice of the time and place thereof to be published, and give notice to parties in interest.

1308.2.3. *Action by the Board, Findings Required.*

The public hearing shall be held, at which any party may appear in person or by agent or attorney. The board shall make its decision within a reasonable time thereafter, not to exceed 30 days.

Before granting any application for a special exception, the board shall make written findings that it is empowered under specified sections of this ordinance to grant the special exception and that the granting of the exception will not adversely affect the public interest. The board shall also make written findings certifying compliance with the specific rules and requirements governing individual special exceptions, and that, where applicable, satisfactory provision and arrangement has been made concerning the following:

(a) Ingress and egress to the property and proposed structures or uses thereon, with particular reference to automotive and pedestrian safety and convenience, traffic flow and control, and access in case of fire or catastrophe.

(b) Off-street parking and loading areas, where required, with particular attention to the items in (a) above.

(c) Refuse and service areas.

(d) Control of noise, glare, odor, or other potentially adverse effects of the proposed use on nearby property, and screening or buffering to alleviate such effects. Control of drainage and erosion.

(e) Utilities, with reference to location, availability and potentially adverse appearance or other effects on surroundings.

(f) Signs and lighting, with reference to glare, traffic safety, and compatibility and harmony with adjoining properties and the character of the area.

(g) Required yards and other open spaces.

Where the special exception is denied, the record of the board shall set forth, and the applicant shall receive notice of, the specific grounds for denial.

1308.2.4. *Conditions and Safeguards.*

The board may impose such conditions relating to the special exception as it may deem necessary in the particular case to protect the public interest, in relation to the items listed at Section 1308.2.3 above and as may otherwise be reasonably necessary, and may require a guarantee or bond to insure continued compliance with such conditions and continued maintenance of such safeguards. Violation of conditions or safeguards lawfully attached to any special exception shall be deemed violations of this ordinance.

1308.2.5. *Special Exceptions Apply to Property, Not Person.*

When granted, a special exception, together with any conditions or safeguards attached, shall apply to the land, structure or use for which it was issued, and not to a particular person.

308.2.6. *Withdrawal of Application; Rehearing if Withdrawn or Denied.*

An application for a special exception may be withdrawn at any time, but if withdrawn after the board has convened the public hearing at which it was to be considered, or if denied by the board, substantially the same application shall not be considered within 24 months from date of withdrawal or denial.

In connection with particular special exceptions, substantive requirements should be as specific as reasonably possible, and matters for special consideration (other than those which have already been covered in the material applying generally) should be indicated with care. As an example of defective practice and an effort toward improvement, the

Atlanta ordinance in effect as this is written handles a child care nursery, pre-kindergarten, kindergarten, play school, or special school under the head of special use permits. Special use permits involve notice and hearing before, and decisions by, the governing body, which in a city the size of Atlanta should probably not be concerning itself with location of kindergartens regardless of where they are proposed—the requirement for special permit applies generally and not in selected districts.

(The current Atlanta ordinance definition of child care nursery is defective in a number of respects, including minimum number of children involved—seven—and maximum age—17. Both are set too high. Between the definition and the special use permit requirement, this type of approval would be required for all elementary and high schools, an unintended result remedied by judicious neglect in administration.)

The proposed definition reads as follows:

Section 1412. *Child Care Nursery.*

This term, which includes day care centers, pre-kindergarten, kindergarten, play, and other special schools or day care facilities for young children (other than at public or private elementary schools having at least four grades, including kindergarten) is to be construed as applying to establishments providing care and maintenance to four or more children separated from their parents or guardians during part of the day between 6 a.m. and 7 p.m. It is not intended to apply to foster homes, group homes, rehabilitation centers, orphanages, or other institutions providing overnight care or primarily for remedial care.

The definition is not specific on upper age limit, but intent is indicated by the term "young children" and the reference to schools with a minimum of four grades, including kindergarten.

Instead of requiring action by the governing body on all proposals for such establishments within city limits proposed provisions call for special exception proceedings in single-family and two-family districts only. Special considerations include prevention of excessive penetration of neighborhoods by traffic on minor streets, safety for children, and peace and tranquility for the neighbors:

Section 1230. *Detailed Requirements on Certain Special Exceptions.*

In addition to requirements elsewhere set forth, the following requirements and limitations shall apply to the uses or structures indicated below, in districts where such uses and structures require special exceptions:

Secton 1321. *Child Care Nurseries, Day Care Centers, and the Like.*

Child care nurseries, day care centers, pre-kindergarten, kindergarten, play, and other special schools or day care facilities for young children shall be subject to the following requirements:

1321.1. *Access.*

Vehicular entrances to the grounds of such establishments shall be within 300 feet of a major or collector street by normal vehicular routes.

1321.2. *Minimum Lot Width and Area.*

Minimum lot width shall be 120 feet, minimum lot area 15,000 square feet, provided that, for purposes of these provisions, minimum lot width requirements shall be considered to be met if the portion of the lot containing the fenced play area required below has the minimum required width at all points, and minimum lot area requirements shall be considered to be met if the fenced play area is on another lot, not separated by a major or collector street from the lot with the principal stucture, and the combined areas of the lots involved meet minimum area requirements.

1321.3. *Fenced Play Areas.*

A fenced play area of not less than 4,000 square feet shall be provided for 20 children or less, with 200 square feet for each additional child. Such play areas shall be so located as to provide maximum peace and tranquility to adjoining residential uses and to protect the safety of the children. No portion of the fenced play area shall be closer than 20 feet to the line of an adjacent lot in a residential district.

1321.4. *Limitation of Hours for Outdoor Play Activities.*

All outdoor play activities on the premises shall be conducted within the fenced play area, and if the fenced play area is within 100 feet of an occupied residence on adjoining property, such activities shall be limited to the hours between 8 a.m. and 6 p.m.

1321.5. *Buffering.*

Where necessary to provide for peace and tranquility of adjoining residential occupants, solid fences or walls and/or vegetative screening may be required between fenced play areas and adjoining lots in residential use.

Variances

There is probably no area of zoning law where higher courts point in so many directions as the field of variances. Local application of suggestions made here should thus be particularly carefully tempered by examination of applicable state enabling legislation and current judicial climate. Both may conflict in some respects with what is said here, and both may be changing rapidly.

Original framers of zoning knew no ordinance could be drawn with such foresight, knowledge, and clarity as to be equitable in all circumstances. The variance was intended as a device for adjustment where the ordinance created unnecessary hardship in unusual cases, to give affected property owners rights as nearly equal as possible to those of others in the same district.

A heavy case load on variances indicates that the ordinance is defective, the board is malfunctioning, or both. The need for variances should be minor, and variances should be granted sparingly.

No zoning ordinance can be perfect, but few need be as imperfect as they are. A patchwork ordinance constructed by unskilled labor with defective tools requires a great deal of adjustment.

Standard Act Provisions v. Florida State Enabling Legislation Limiting Rules[2]

Under the Standard Act, the third power of the board is "to authorize upon appeal in specific cases such variance from the terms of the ordinance as will not be contrary to the public interest, where, owing to special conditions, a literal enforcement of the provisions of the ordinance will result in unnecessary hardship, and so that the spirit of the ordinance shall be observed and substantial justice done."

Florida Statutes, Chapter 163, Part II, represent a distillation of some of the more important court interpretations concerning this language. At Section 163.225(3)(a) the board is empowered:

To authorize upon appeal such variance from the terms of the ordinance as will not be contrary to the public interest when, owing to special conditions, a literal enforcement of the provisions of the ordinance would result in unnecessary and undue hardship. In order to authorize any variance from the terms of the ordinance, the board of adjustment must find:

1. That special conditions and circumstances exist which are peculiar to the land, structure, or building involved and which are not applicable to other lands, structures, or buildings in the same zoning district;

2. That the special conditions and circumstances do not result from the actions of the applicant;

3. That granting the variance requested will not confer on the applicant any special privilege that is denied by this ordinance to other lands, buildings, or structures in the same zoning district;

4. That literal interpretation of the provisions of the ordinance would deprive the applicant of rights commonly enjoyed by other properties in the same zoning district under the terms of the ordinance and would work unnecessary and undue hardship on the applicant;

5. That the variance granted is the minimum variance that will make possible the reasonable use of the land, building, or structure;

6. That the grant of the variance will be in harmony with the general intent and purpose of the ordinance and that such variance will not be

injurious to the area involved or otherwise detrimental to the public welfare.

(b) In granting any variance, the board of adjustment may prescribe appropriate conditions and safeguards in conformity with this part and any ordinance enacted under its authority. Violation of such conditions and safeguards, when made a part of the terms under which the variance is granted, shall be deemed a violation of the ordinance.

(c) The board of adjustment may prescribe a reasonable time limit within which the action for which the variance is required shall be begun or completed or both.

(d) Under no circumstances except as permitted above shall the board of adjustment grant a variance to permit a use not generally or by special exception permitted in the zoning district involved or any use expressly or by implication prohibited by the terms of the ordinance in the zoning district. No nonconforming use of neighboring lands, structures, or buildings in the same zoning district and no permitted use of lands, structures, or buildings in other zoning districts shall be considered grounds for the authorization of a variance.

Other states have been adding similar guidelines to enabling legislation, and local ordinances increasingly contain such requirements for specific findings or limitations on the use of variance powers.

New Jersey, in its enabling legislation (Title 40, Section 55–39, New Jersey Statutes), closes the door to use variances by the board at subsection (c), but opens it again by an action having the same effect at subsection (d), with one important difference. The board may "recommend in particular cases and for special reasons to the governing body . . . the granting of a variance to allow a structure or use in a district restricted against such structures or uses." Here the board merely recommends, and the governing body issues what is in effect a special permit.

About the best that can be said for such a procedure is that the governing body and the board establish a checks and balances system in which the governing body has the upper hand. If the board recommends a use variance for "special reasons" (whatever those might be—the language is loose), the governing body may or may not grant it, which isn't quite the same technically as spot zoning, although it certainly has the same effect. If the board decides not to recommend, the governing body can go ahead and spot zone anyway.[3]

Corollary Guidelines
In addition to the limiting rules laid down above in Florida legislation, other states and local ordinance provisions spell out some other guides

which are at least in part implicit in Florida language. Among these are the following:

A variance is not the appropriate remedy for a general condition. In effect, the proposed Atlanta ordinance, at 1308.3.2(b) and (d), restates the first item in the Florida act:

(b) Such hardship is not shared generally by other properties in the same district and the same vicinity.

(d) The condition or situation of the property is not of so general or recurring a nature as to make reasonably practicable the formulation of a general regulation to be adopted as an amendment to the ordinance. (In such cases, the secretary of the board shall take steps to initiate consideration of such an amendment.)[4]

Self-inflected hardship is not grounds for a variance. This restates item two of the Florida strictures. If a man with a lot sufficiently large for uses permitted in the district sells off a portion to a neighbor, diminishing remaining frontage or areas below that required for a use permitted in the district, he is not entitled to a variance on grounds of the hardship he brought on himself. In contrast, if the area or width of the lot was reduced because land was taken for street widening, the hardship is not self-inflicted. (He may not be entitled to a variance anyway, if a similar reduction has been created all along the street frontage, but here there should be a remedy in other ordinance language discussed at pages 43–45.)

Personal hardship is not grounds for variance. The hardship must relate to the physical character of the property. This is implicit in item one of the Florida legislation: The special conditions and circumstances must be "peculiar to the land, structure, or building involved."

The proposed Atlanta ordinance makes the rule explicit, and gives reasons for it, in setting forth findings which must be made by the board before granting a variance at Section 1308.3.2:

(c) The hardship is created by the physical character of the property, including dimensions, topography, or soil conditions, or by other extraordinary situation or condition of such property. Personal hardship shall not be considered as grounds for a variance, since the variance will continue to affect the character of the neighborhood after title to the property has passed.

The Atlanta ordinance well states the purpose of the personal hardship rule. As an extreme example of its violation, the writer shortly after World War II came across a board composed of compassionate citizens aware of their debt to the armed forces. It had a policy of allowing any use variance requested by a disabled veteran of the recent conflict. Requests included automotive repair and body work at homes in residential areas, groceries in the front rooms of residences, and the like. The intent concerning the individuals involved were benign, but the effects on their neighborhoods were malignant.

Economic hardship in itself is not grounds for a variance.   It may be considered as an element, but there must be other compelling considerations. Williams states the rule thus:

> In general, the law guarantees that police power measures will not prevent a property owner from obtaining some reasonable return on his land, however that may be defined. . . . One of the most common statements in variance law is that purely financial hardship—i.e., restriction to a less profitable use—is not sufficient to justify a variance. Statements on this point recur with great frequency all through the law on variances, both in cases upholding denial of a variance sought on this basis and in cases upsetting variances granted with no more justification than this.[5]

The Loudoun County, Virginia, ordinance currently in effect recognizes this limitation at Section 1106.2.2, *Exceptional Narrowness, Shallowness, Size, etc.*, by requiring the board to be satisfied, "upon the evidence heard by it, that the granting of such variance will alleviate a clearly *demonstrable hardship approaching confiscation,* as distinguished from a special privilege or convenience sought by the application. . . ."

There are several sound reasons for this position. Economic hardship is personal, rather than arising from the physical condition of the property. It is often self-inflicted. An applicant having paid too high a price for land and aware of the zoning limitations on it is not entitled to a variance which will enable him to get what he considers an appropriate return, based on the price paid.

As in the case of most appeals for variances based on personal hardship, if the variance is granted, the temporary plight of the appellant may be relieved, but the effect on the neighborhood is long-lasting.

The hardship must be severe and unnecessary in achieving public purposes.   All zoning restricts use of property, and to that extent might be construed as creating a hardship. As stated at item four of Florida legislation, it is only where zoning works "unnecessary and undue" hardship on the applicant that a variance is justified, and then only when other requirements are met.

The variance shall not adversely affect adjacent property or the character of the district.   This limitation is implicit in item six of the

Florida statute but might well be spelled out either in enabling legislation or in local ordinances, as in Norfolk's controls at Section 803.2(c), which prohibits issuance of a variance unless the board finds: "that the authorization of such variance will not be of substantial detriment to adjacent property and that the character of the district will not be changed by the granting of the variance."

The "Whitnall rule" on equal rights. Items three and four in the Florida limiting rules state that applicants are not to receive special privileges denied generally in the district, and that they must be denied rights enjoyed by others before the variance may be granted.[6]

Gordon Whitnall, respected zoning authority, used the following diagram in illustrating the principles involved:

At A, all rights are equal, and no variance is justified. At B, a variance allowing special privilege should not be allowed. At C, one owner, owing to unusual circumstances, is deprived of rights applying generally. A variance is in order, but only to the extent of allowing equal rights.

Notes

1. Frederick H. Bair, Jr., "Boards of Adjustment and How They Got That Way," in *Planning Cities* (Chicago: American Society of Planning Officials, 1970), p. 486.

2. The Florida provisions are substantially the same as those suggested for local ordinances in *Text of a Model Zoning Ordinance, With Commentary*, published in first edition by the Public Administration Clearing Service of the University of Florida in 1958, and in the second (1960) and third (1966) editions by the American Society of Planning Officials (cf. p. 53, 3rd ed.). A substantial number of ordinances now include similar language and some are even more specific on prohibition of use variances. Thus, the Columbia, South Carolina, zoning ordinance effective March 18, 1963, states at Section 320.03(f): "With respect to uses of land, buildings and other structures, this ordinance is declared to be a definition of the public interest by City Council, and the spirit of this ordinance will not be observed by any variance which permits a use not generally or by

special exception permitted in the district involved, or any uses expressly or by implication prohibited by the terms of this ordinance in said district."

3. On this point, see Norman J. Williams, Jr., *American Land Planning Law* (Chicago: Callaghan and Co., 1974) Vol. 1, §138.03 "*c*" and "*d*", and Robert M. Anderson, *American Law of Zoning* (Rochester, N.Y.: Lawyers Cooperative Publishing Co., 1976), §14.15. Williams comes down hard on the practice; Anderson is more temperate in his comments but may be less accurate in his appraisal of the effects.

4. This charge to the board need not be included in enabling legislation but takes a positive step in assuring that potential improvements in the ordinance will at least be examined. It doesn't help the applicant with a meritorious case to tell him that a variance cannot be granted because the same thing is happening all over the jurisdiction due to discernible defects in the ordinance. It *would* help him if, following denial, he was assured that steps would be initiated to remedy the deficiency.

5. Williams, *American Land Planning Law*, §143.04, "A Greater Financial Return?"

6. Obviously, this must be broadly construed. A variance reducing a yard requirement for reasons of unusual topography obviously extends a special privilege. Others are not permitted to have yards of such lesser dimensions. But if without the variance the appellant could not build a residence in a district in which similar residences are permitted, the grant merely gives him equal status on this point.

3
Exercises in the Application of Principles Concerning Variances

In the best of all possible zoning worlds, governed by the ideal ordinance, the upright and intelligent board would never have a variance appeal before it. Rules in the ordinance would cover every conceivable situation, drawing firm lines between what is permitted by right with specified conditions and safeguards to protect well-defined public interest and what is not permitted because it infringes that interest.

Where this ideal is not achieved, there should be movement toward it. The vigor of the movement, and rewards to expect from it, should vary directly according to the size of the case load. Reduction of the board's burden, while a desirable objective, is not the primary purpose of the exercise. The main goal is to benefit the public by permitting as a matter of right all that can be allowed without damage to public objectives, and eliminating needless procedural ceremonials.

Cases below illustrate application of these principles to variance practice. Where specific standards are set in these rules (as in the case of the 80 percent rule), they are merely illustrative and should be modified to reflect local circumstances (including local tolerance).

Where to begin and how to proceed? Look for a pattern of meritorious appeals based on unusual (but not unique) hardships. What ordinance amendment will cure the largest part of them without undermining public purposes?

Stated differently, relief through variance should be granted only where there are unique circumstances. The dockets of many boards are loaded because they grant variance appeals based on hardships which are merely uncommon. Admittedly, this exceeds the strict-construction powers of the board, but it does happen as a matter of practice. The cure—write rules into the ordinance covering the class or classes of cases involved, providing as a matter of right such relief as would be appropriate through sympathetic but illegal variance. This lightens the case load and conscience of the board. It also removes the burden of those who would otherwise have to apply for a variance the board should not grant for an action which should be permitted.

The Case of the Adjoining Nonconforming Lots

The ordinance provides that on single lots of record with area or width below that required in the district, a single-family residence may be built, provided yard requirements are met. If yard requirements cannot be met, a variance is required.

Where two or more lots of record adjoin in continuous frontage and ownership, and all or part of such lots do not meet ordinance requirements for width or area, the land shall be considered an undivided parcel. No portion shall be used or sold in a manner which diminishes compliance with the ordinance or creates a lot width or area less than required.

The purpose of these requirements is to permit use of single nonconforming lots, but to require combination and resubdivision into conforming lots where the ownership pattern makes this possible.

Comes now Attorney Glibwise for a variance, and sets forth the following circumstances:

His client, Mrs. Smith, is the widow of the late Hector Smith, who will be remembered by members of the board as the genial proprietor of Hector's Coffee Shop and a willing volunteer in service club activities. Mrs. Smith is in frail health and precarious financial circumstances.

Prior to enactment of the zoning ordinance, the late Mr. Smith purchased three adjoining lots facing on Pine Street. A residence was erected in the center of this property, leaving two vacant lots at the sides which were used for a flower garden and a vegetable garden. Mrs. Smith now finds herself unable to maintain these and would like to sell them. Mr. Smith had always anticipated building on them for rental property but was unable to do so before his long and agonizing death from cancer. Mrs. Smith is virtually destitute as a result of payment of his medical bills and final expenses and is herself in need of a series of operations.

In addition to humanitarian reasons for granting the variance (or variances if the board elects to handle each lot individually), there is an injustice to be corrected here. The ordinance calls for a 60-foot minimum width, and the lots are only 50 feet wide. Strict application of the regula-tions requires Mrs. Smith to maintain 150 feet of frontage, two and a half times the minimum for the district. To prohibit the sale of the two lots, or their use for construction, is obviously confiscatory—no use allowable in the district can be made of the individual lots. No court in the land would uphold denial of the variance, says Counselor Glibwise, and he cites a number of cases which are superficially similar in support of his position.

Since court reversal of a board denial is virtually certain, the board can see the unfairness of subjecting Mrs. Smith (in her straitened cir-cumstances) to the added expense of an appeal.

A report from the Planning Department is considered at this point. In the general area involved, subdivision took place in the twenties, and most of the lots are 50 feet in width. The area is fairly well built-up, with a significant proportion of residences being built on two- or three-lot combinations, some in the pattern of Mrs. Smith's, with the dwelling on a single lot and a lot at the side or at each side.

The 60-foot minimum applies generally within the R–2 district in which the property is located. This minimum is desirable because most land lying within R–2 districts is platted in 60-foot lots, and a considerable area remains unsubdivided. The future pattern of these tracts should in-volve the 60-foot minimum width.

Neighbors voice their opinions, generally strongly favorable to Mrs. Smith's case.

Given this scenario, what action should the board take?

It may be difficult to exclude from consideration Mrs. Smith's physical and economic decline or memories of the genial Hector, but it should be done. Personal and financial hardships (and even nostalgia) should be played down.

There is hardship. It is not self-inflicted. It is difficult to believe that it could be construed as a *necessary* hardship, considering purposes of the ordinance.

It seems a rank injustice to require Mrs. Smith to maintain a frontage two and a half times the minimum for the district. Considering the com-ponent lots individually, it seems clearly confiscatory to prohibit building on two of them. Under the ordinance, however, they are not to be con-strued as three lots, but as one parcel, and for that parcel there is a reasonable use.

The Planning Department's report indicates that the problem, while not general, is also not uncommon in the area.

Granting the variance would not confer a special privilege on the applicant, in the sense that it would allow the erection of single-family dwellings on individual lots that are nonconforming as to width. In single ownership, this would be a use by right in the district. On the other hand, the ordinance has specifically foreseen the possibility of such combinations and the opportunity to bring about resubdivision and reduce nonconformity. In this light, granting the variance would confer a special privilege and undermine the purposes of the ordinance.

The opinion of the neighbors, while it may be considered, should not be a weighty element in reaching a decision. When boards give undue weight to such opinion, getting a variance depends on the kind of neighbors the appellant has, rather than on the equities involved.

The character of the neighborhood would not be adversely affected. As indicated by the Planning Department's report, most lots in the area are 50 feet in width and are occupied by single-family houses.

Given this array of considerations, the board should not grant the variance. This course, if matters stop there, will send its members home feeling righteous and miserable. If they grant the variance, they will feel guilty and warm, having dispensed mercy rather than justice. But matters need not stop there. The board can set in motion remedial action that will solve Mrs. Smith's problem without granting her a variance, and help a lot of other people as well (including the board, by reducing its future work load).

It seems fairly obvious that it is the ordinance which needs adjustment, and, since the board discovered the deficiency, the board should suggest it. As noted earlier, this is not a duty assigned by law but an action dictated by common sense.

Why was an extensive built-up area with a 50-foot pattern zoned for 60-foot lot widths in the first place? Character was established and is unlikely to be changed by the greater lot-width requirement. An easy and fairly simple solution might well be to suggest surrounding such enclaves with their own boundaries and making them R–2A districts, with the same general regulations as for R–2, except for a minimum lot width of 50 feet, rather than 60. The board might well make such a recommendation.

The Norfolk Solution—The 80 Percent Rule

As a supplementary solution, or an alternate to such a proposal to apply where situations of the kind described do not cover substantial areas, it might be helpful to provide rules in the ordinance governing combinations of nonconforming lots, to allow minor adjustments without board action.

In Norfolk, Virginia, in 1968, a case with circumstances paralleling those of Mrs. Smith led to both a split in a previous single district and the following language applying generally. Article VII, *Nonconformities*, now contains this provision:

Section 702. *Combinations of Lots and Portions of Lots.*

If a lot or portion of a lot or two or more lots or combinations of lots and portions of lots, with continuous frontage in single ownership, are of record at the time of passage of this amendment of this ordinance, and if all or part of the lots do not meet the requirements established for lot width and area, the following rules shall apply:

702.1. *80 Percent Rule Applicable in All Cases Concerning Three Lots or Less.*

Where such lot, portion of lot, or combination consists of sufficient width and area to provide at least 80 percent of the width and area generally required for three lots or less in the district, the land may be divided for use into three lots or less, each of which shall have at least 80 percent of the lot width and area generally required in the district.

702.2. *Rule for Other Multiple Lots Not Covered by Section 702.1 Above.*

Where such lot, portion of lot, or combination consists of greater width or area than generally required for creation of three lots, the land shall be divided for use into lots all of which conform to the lot width and area generally required in the district, provided, however, that in such division one remaining lot may be created having not less than 80 percent of the lot width and area generally required in the district or that reduction equivalent in total to such reduction on a remaining lot may be distributed between the divisions created.

702.3. *Prohibition Against Creation of Other Lots Below Width and Area Requirements for District.*

Other than as provided herein by Sections 702.1 and 702.2, no lot or parcel or portion thereof shall be used or sold in a manner diminishing compliance with lot width and area requirements established by this ordinance, nor shall any division be made in accordance with the subdivision regulations which creates a lot with width or area below the requirements stated in this ordinance.

Here, in addition to solving the problems of those in the situation of Mrs. Smith, the ordinance makes provision for general minor variation in order to handle cases involving more than three adjoining lots where a remainder would be slightly less than the full amount generally required.

Two Cases on Substandard Lots Created by Public Action, and Some Related Considerations

A Single Lot

Jones owns a vacant residential lot of required (and substantial) dimensions). The school board, expanding the school grounds, wants part of it. Jones sells voluntarily. He knows that the board can exercise eminent domain and has done so in the past.

Both adjoining lots are also of required dimensions, with little to spare, and both are developed. The school board needs land only from Jones.[1]

The sales to the school board leaves Jones with a substandard lot, but under the current definition in the ordinance it is not legally "nonconforming,"[2] so Jones can't build on it without a variance as things now stand.

The ordinance contains the usual prohibition against selling any portion of a lot which creates a remnant of less than required dimensions. It also disallows self-inflicted hardship as grounds for a variance.

Jones seeks a variance. This puts both Jones and the board astride a high fence. He sold "voluntarily" but under imminent threat of use of eminent domain proceedings. Was it a self-inflicted hardship? The ordinance prohibited the sale, and Jones is technically in violation. Violation of the ordinance is hardly grounds for a variance. Should Jones have insisted that the school board take his entire lot or none of it, citing the ordinance requirement? Should he have refused to sell voluntarily, forcing condemnation so that the violation of the zoning ordinance would, in effect, have been at the order of the court?

Robert M. Anderson states a generally recognized rule that, "where an applicant for a variance can demonstrate that owing to the size and shape of his land he cannot make any reasonable use of it unless the literal application of the zoning regulations is varied, he is entitled to a variance."[3] He also states another generally recognized rule: "In most jurisdictions, an applicant whose problems in the use of his land are caused by his own conduct, rather than by circumstances which are peculiarly related to the land, is not entitled to an area variance."[4]

Is Jones entitled to a variance? A hard-nosed board may say no, a more sympathetic board yes. But if the ordinance is drafted to handle this kind of situation, the board will not become embroiled in such decisions. Remedial action is suggested following the next case, which involves a series of lots reduced to substandard status by public action.

This raises another point concerning the Jones situation. While it is true that only a single lot is involved here, the hard-nosed board, in denying Jones his variance, might well buttress its position by pointing out that Jones's condition falls in so general a class of cases as to make "reasonably practicable the formulation of a general regulation to be adopted as an amendment to the ordinance," as provided specifically in the ordinance language suggested on page 43, and as reasonably implied from the general rule that the conditions must be special, peculiar to the property, and not applicable to other properties in the same district.

A Series of Lots

Mountain Drive is widened through the entire Lofty Oaks subdivision, removing many of the oaks and 15 feet of front yards of developed property on both sides. (The front yard depth requirement is 25 feet.) The original developer of Lofty Oaks, a thrifty person, laid out the lots at the minimum width and area required by the zoning ordinance. Most lots are occupied, but some remain vacant. Some owners sold voluntarily. Others yielded only to condemnation proceedings.

Edelweiss seeks to build a residence on his single lot, which is now substandard but not, under the current definition, nonconforming. Denied a permit, he seeks a variance on lot area requirements and on front yard requirements, pointing out that, owing to the actions of a benign government (which he was powerless to avert during condemnation proceedings), he now does not have the required amount of land, that he can't acquire more from his neighbors, and that, if he provides the required front yard, his rear yard (the only usable private open space on his lot) will be only 15 feet in depth. As an added argument, he observes that his neighbors on both sides now have front yards only 10 feet deep. He claims an equal right or privilege (if that's what it is). Edelweiss is not happy about the benefits accruing to traffic circulation at his expense, nor about having to go through all this red tape.

He will not be happy when the board turns down his requests for variance, either, but that's what the board should do. The problem (and the hardship) is general, and not unique to his property. Whether the hardships involved are self-inflicted or government-inflicted is not the main issue in this case.

Some Related Considerations on the Taking of Land for Public Purposes

Thus far, in this pair of cases, the situations have involved governmental actions (a) reducing the area of an individual lot, and (b) reducing both lots and existing yards. Where the front yard was reduced, portions of buildings extending beyond the new 25-foot setback are technically in violation of the ordinance under the standard definition of nonconforming structures. (The yards were reduced *after* the regulations went into effect.)

There are other instances where such taking of land for public purposes and related actions on installation of improvements may create unnecessary problems for property owners (and perhaps for the board) unless the ordinance is constructed to handle them. Not all of these are related to the hypothetical cases discussed above, but coordinated treatment seems in order.

Ordinances usually prohibit reduction of off-street parking below minimums required and often prohibit resumption of nonconforming uses after specified periods of abandonment. Many ordinances contain amortization provisions, specifying maximum length of time certain nonconforming uses may continue.

Comes now a street-widening project which reduces required off-street parking, or street or other governmental construction which impedes access to the premises of a nonconforming use. The ordinance should make some provision so that it does not create technical violations by the actions of government, or cause the clock to run on abandonment or amortization during the period which government action makes normal use impossible. The board might become involved in a number of variance (or other) cases here unless the regulations cover such contingencies.

Remedial Ordinance Provisions, Atlanta
Taking these problems approximately in the order in which they have been discussed, a proposed Atlanta ordinance deals with them as follows:

Lots and yards. Under the general head *Application of Regulations*, Atlanta language varies from usual provisions by including the words "by private action":

220.3. *Lots and Yards to Meet Minimum Requirements; Reduction Below Minimum Requirements by Private Action Prohibited.*

Lots and yards created after the effective date of regulations related thereto shall meet the minimum requirements set forth therein, and no lot or yard existing at the effective date of such regulations shall thereafter be reduced by private action below the minimums set forth therein. (For effect of *reduction in area* by public action, see Section 1102, *Nonconforming Lots of Record;* for effect of reduction of *yards* by public action, see Section 1325, *Special Exceptions on Yards Where Adjacent Existing Yards on Developed Property Are Reduced Below Minimum Requirements by Public Action,* and Section 1107, *Nonconforming Structures*).

Following through on the cross-references, Section 1102 adds to the usual language defining nonconforming lots of record an indication that substandard lots created by public taking shall also be construed as nonconforming:

Section 1102. *Nonconforming Lots of Record.*

Where legal lots of record at the time of passage or amendment of this ordinance have dimensions below the minimum requirements established by such regulations, regulations and requirements applying thereto shall be as provided below. In cases where land is taken for public purposes from legal lots of record at the time of such taking, the lots remaining shall also be construed to be nonconforming lots of record, and subject to the same regulations and restrictions.[5]

Section 1325. *Special Exceptions on Yards Where Adjacent Existing Yards Are Reduced Below Minimum Requirements by Public Action.*

Where land acquisition for public purposes reduces existing yards on developed properties adjacent to or near and in logical relation to properties which are vacant and to be developed, or properties to be redeveloped, the Board, as a special exception, may reduce applicable yard requirements on the property to be developed or redeveloped, subject to the following considerations and limitations:

(a) Such reduction shall not result in a yard requirement less than the average of yards of generally required dimensions or less on developed property adjacent or nearest to the lot affected. In making such computations, yards on developed properties separated from the lot affected by a street or alley shall not be included, nor shall yards of greater dimension than required by general regulation. In such cases, the factor to be included in averaging shall be the full yard dimension generally required.

(b) No such reduction shall amount to more than 60 percent of the requirement generally applicable.

(c) The maximum allowable reduction may be lowered for adequate cause stated in the findings, as for example where it is determined that there is reasonable likelihood that adjoining or nearby buildings involved in computations of average yard requirement are likely to be removed and the property redeveloped in the near future, or where such maximum allowable reduction would result in hazards to persons or traffic by reason of inadequate visibility.

Nonconforming Structures. The technical violations created by the taking (with portions of structures extending into required yards reduced by governmental action) are cured by the same general approach as was used on nonconforming lots:

Section 1107. *Nonconforming Structures.*

Where a lawful structure or portion thereof becomes nonconforming by reason of adoption or amendment of this ordinance, and could not be built under its terms by reason of restrictions imposed on area, lot coverage, height, yards, location on the lot, or other requirements concerning the structure, such structure or portion thereof may be continued so long as it is and remains otherwise lawful, subject to the provisions set forth below. In cases where land is taken for public purposes from legal lots of record at the time of such taking in such a manner as to reduce yards previously provided in relation to a portion of a structure below yard requirements generally applicable within the district, the portion of the structure involved shall be construed to be nonconforming.

(Here follow provisions on structural change, alteration or expansion, reconstruction in case of damage, and moving.)

On reduction of required off-street parking or loading space by public action, Atlanta remedies are as follows:

220.4. *Reduction of Required Off-Street Parking or Loading Space.*

No existing off-street parking or loading space, and no off-street parking or loading space hereafter provided, which meets all or part of the requirements for off-street parking or loading space set forth in these regulations, shall be reduced or eliminated by *private action* unless no longer required by these regulations, or unless alternative parking or loading space meeting the requirements of these regulations is provided. (For effect of reduction by public action, see Section 1109, *Nonconforming Characteristics of Use.*) (Emphasis supplied.)

Potential nonconforming characteristics of use include a number of things, of which only parking and loading are likely to be affected by public taking:

1109. *Nonconforming Characteristics of Use.*

If accessory characteristics of use, such as signs, off-street parking and loading, lighting, or other matters pertaining to the use of land, structures, or premises are made nonconforming by this ordinance as passed or amended, no change shall be made which increases the degree of nonconformity with the requirements of this ordinance, but change may be made which results in the same or a lesser degree of nonconformity. In cases where land is taken for public purposes in such a manner as to reduce off-street parking or loading space below that previously existing and required by the regulations for the district, the deficiency thus created shall be construed as a nonconforming characteristic of use.

Concerning discontinuance and amortization provisions, all that is necessary is to include, in stating times involved, "except during periods when governmental action materially impedes access to the premises."

The Case of the Unwise Investor and the Highest and Best Use

Corbett, a petroleum products dealer, purchased a lot he felt was superbly located for a gas station site, at the intersection of two major streets. He paid a very high price for it. The general area is zoned to permit apartments, motels, restaurants, and some other service uses, but not gas stations. To remedy this difficulty, Corbett seeks a variance.

Arguments in support of the grant of variance are extensive and buttressed by expert testimony:

1. Filling stations are not authorized in the district; Corbett's land is worth much more for a filling station than for authorized purposes, and the difference in value and potential income resulted in unique hardship justifying the granting of a variance. Use of the land for a filling station constitutes the "highest and best" use.

2. Three corners of the intersection are already occupied by motels. Placing a motel on the fourth would add to congestion and accident potentials. A gas station, on the other hand, would leave a large visibility triangle and lessen traffic hazards, thus promoting public welfare and safety.

3. Because of the size and shape of the lot, a motel would not fit well on it. The ordinance authorizes variances where the size and shape of the lot create practical difficulties or unnecessary hardships.

4. In the location proposed, and constructed as planned, the gas station would not diminish the value of surrounding property.

Convinced by these arguments, the board grants the variance. What is wrong with the decision? Quite a number of things:

1. The applicant knew when he purchased the land that gas stations were not permitted in the district. Self-inflicted hardship is not grounds for a variance.

2. The "highest and best use," as appraisers and realtors use the term, is that which will yield the greatest financial returns. One reason we have zoning is that uses which yield the highest financial returns cause trouble if they are located in the wrong places.

3. A variance requires demonstration of unique hardship relating to the character of the land. Corbett's hardship relates to paying too

much for land he couldn't use for the purpose he intended. Neither cupidity nor stupidity entitles to a variance.

4. Any hardship inherent in prohibition of gas stations within the district is general. Neither Corbett's lot nor any other may be used for gas stations. Corbett thus was asking for a special privilege not extended to others similarly situated. The variance violated the "Whitnall rule" on equal rights.

5. The argument that three corners are occupied by motels, so the fourth should *not* be, is a reversal of a standard ploy. Usually, in filling station cases, an attempt is made to justify added filling stations at an intersection because one or more corners are already occupied by filling stations. In any case, the safety argument, while superficially attractive, has nothing to do with the merits of Corbett's appeal for a variance. While the board might well attach to a variance conditions to promote safety, it should not grant an illegal variance on grounds that the proposed use will be safer than one which is permitted.

6. Going even farther afield from central issues (so far as legitimate arguments are concerned), Corbett demonstrated that he couldn't use his lot as profitably for a motel as for a gas station. The district allows a number of other uses, including apartments and restaurants. Corbett did not prove that he could not use his lot for *any* of the other allowable purposes, so that it could hardly be claimed that the ordinance was confiscatory as applied to his land.

7. The allegation that the gas station, as proposed, would not be likely to diminish the value of surrounding property is incidental at best, so far as the issues in this case are concerned. Presumably uses permitted in the district would not diminish the value of surrounding property either.

What the board did here was to amend the ordinance in the guise of granting a variance. This it was not empowered to do. Had the governing body amended the ordinance to permit a gas station on this lot, it would have been within the limits of its powers, but they would have been wrongfully applied, since the action would clearly have been "spot zoning," the singling out of a small piece of land for special treatment for reasons not related to the public purposes of zoning.

In a case closely parallel to that described here, on appeal the high court said in part:[6]

To endow such a board with the authority to amend the zoning ordinance in particular instances by authorizing a use of property prohibited in the ordinance . . . would be to convey to the appeals board the authority to enact legislation, nullify the decision of the municipal legislative body, and in effect destroy the beneficent results to be obtained by comprehensive zoning.

Notes

1. The taking pattern assumed here affects one lot only and seems hard on Jones but keeps analysis of the case simpler. We want to make it clear that there is no way he can buy land from his neighbors. For those who seek complications, see Robert M. Anderson, *American Law of Zoning* (Rochester, N.Y.: Lawyers Cooperative Publishing Co., 1976), §8.49 and §14.51, or Norman J. Williams, *American Land Planning Law* (Chicago: Callaghan and Co., 1974), Vol. 1, §41.01 and §41.02. Williams's chart on "Existing Small or Narrow Lots—Analyses of Various Situations, and Alternative Courses of Action Available" is particularly illuminating as to potentials, although he does not cover the case of Mrs. Smith, as discussed previously.

2. Here we have another zoning language problem. A "conforming" lot meets area and width requirements. Logic would indicate that a "nonconforming" lot is one that does not, but the usual definition is narrower than this. A nonconforming lot is one that was of record and legal at the time ordinance requirements required greater dimensions. A lot that was not of record or had been illegally created at the time the requirements were established is not considered a nonconforming lot. Neither is a lot that is reduced below the required minimum after the requirements were established. Such lots are usually termed "substandard," a generic term that also includes nonconforming lots.

3. Anderson, *American Law of Zoning*, Vol. 3, §14.51, p. 20.

4. Anderson, *American Law of Zoning*, §14.53, p. 27.

5. This provision also would get Jones off the hook unless the pattern of taking *on his individual lot* makes it impossible for him to build with the full yard dimensions generally required, in which case a variance of the yard requirements might be appropriate. In situations such as that described for Lofty Oaks, variances are not the approved solution, since a substantial number of similar cases are involved. If the matter is not handled by establishing a special district with reduced lot and yard requirements, it might be treated:

(a) By a rule in general regulations establishing yard requirements on undeveloped or redeveloped property as, for example, "the average of similar yards remaining on adjoining developed lots, if both are developed, or the average of the similar yards remaining on an adjoining developed lot and the full yard requirement generally applicable in the district, provided, however, that in no case shall such requirements be reduced to less than 60 percent of the requirement generally applicable;

    (b) By special administrative permit;

    (c) By special exception. Atlanta chose this course because of the effects on the neighborhoods and surrounding property.

    6. *Josephson v. Autrey,* 96 So.2d 784 (1957, Fla.).

4
Rules of the Board;
Models with Commentary

Rules of the Board as Related to Laws Governing the Board

The board is governed in its organization and operation by its own rules—and by general law, state zoning enabling legislation, and the zoning ordinance. In some places, the package is even thicker. In Wisconsin counties, for example, the governing body is required to adopt rules of conduct for the board, and the board may adopt further rules.[1]

If the board is to perform properly—and avoid embarrassment in the courts—its members must be aware of the responsibilities set forth in these sources and of limitations and guidelines concerning them. The board is a quasi-judicial body. As such, it should be familiar with the field of law in which it operates and respect it.

The board, and preferably each of its members, should have a kit including not only the rules it has adopted, but also pertinent state legislation and local ordinances, discussed more fully below.

What follows here is a guided tour of state or local laws likely to affect the board and models from which the board may fashion its own rules.

Standard Act Language and Variations

Standard Act language affecting rules comes from the congested and confusing Section 7, elements of which are analyzed below. Substantial changes have been made in this material by many states, and its is highly important to relate rules to legislation for the particular state involved.

Appointments, Terms, Removals, Vacancies

Such local legislative body may provide for the appointment of a board of adjustment.

This language does not limit the act of appointment to the governing body. In some enabling legislation the governing body is not the appointing authority. In Virginia, for example, state law requires appointment by appropriate courts because of the quasi-judicial character of most board actions.[2] In Alaska, governing bodies serve as boards of adjustment, but cities may delegate part or all board functions to boroughs (equivalent to counties).[3]

Here variations run in all directions: overlapping terms, terms of different lengths, number of members, provisions for alternates, membership qualifications (usually limited to the requirement that members be qualified electors), prohibition against holding other public office in the jurisdiction (except that in some cases a member of the planning commission may be appointed—a good device for liaison), and provisions concerning compensation and staff.

However basic legislation is framed, if it provides for removal for cause and does not indicate the nature of the cause, board rules might well do so. This is usually not handled in the ordinance.

Rules

The board shall adopt rules in accordance with the provisions of any ordinance adopted pursuant to this act.

On this element, variations are minimal. The Wisconsin exception, where the governing body in counties adopts rules for the board, has already been noted.

Meetings; Officers; Administering Oaths; Compelling Attendance of Witnesses; All Meetings to Be Public

Meetings of the board shall be held at the call of the chairman and at such other times as the board may determine. Such chairman, or in his absence the acting chairman, may administer oaths and compel the attendance of witnesses. All meetings of the board shall be open to the public.

Records

The board shall keep minutes of its proceedings, showing the vote of each member upon each question or, if absent or failing to vote, indicating such fact, and shall keep records of its examinations and other official actions, all of which shall be immediately filed in the office of the board and shall be a public record.

There is little important variation between states on the two elements above.

Appeals, How Taken

Appeals to the board of adjustment may be taken by any person aggrieved or by any officer, department, board, or bureau of the municipality affected by any decision of the administrative officer. Such appeal shall be taken within a limited time, as provided by the rules of the board, by filing with the officer from whom the appeal is taken and with the board of adjustment a notice of appeal specifying the grounds thereof. The officer from whom the appeal is taken shall forthwith transmit to the board all the papers constituting the record upon which the action appealed from was taken.

At this point, if the state enabling act or the zoning ordinance has not unscrambled Standard Act language (fitting the pieces together where they belong), rules of the board, if constructed prudently, may make up the deficiency without running afoul of the clear intent of the law. The elements should be rearranged in the order used at page 20, *Appeals from Decisions of Administrative Officials.*

(Much of the material brought together and reordered as indicated was scattered through the Standard Act in a way that led strict constructionists in early years to hold that the board could act on a variance or special exception only after the administrative official had denied a permit. Reason has now generally prevailed. The administrative official is powerless to issue a variance, and an application for a special exception is not an appeal. In such cases, there is no purpose in requiring application for and denial of a permit that cannot legally be issued as an initial step toward variance or special exception actions.

There is an interesting Catch 22 if strict constructionism is followed to its tortuous conclusion. In the Standard act, board powers to hear and decide appeals on allegations of error, applications for special exception, and appeals for variances are listed ahead of the provision that the board have all the powers of the officer from whom the appeal is taken. But the officer doesn't have the power to authorize special exceptions or grant variances in the first place. Under the strict construction approach, that's why he had to deny the initial application for a permit.

To complicate matters further—which hardly seems desirable at this juncture—starting the clock on time limitations for action on special exceptions and variances at the time of denial of a futile application for a permit penalizes all concerned. Time limits on actions on variance and special exception decisions should start from the point at which a completed appeal or application is received.)

Public Notice and Hearing; Parties May Appear in Person, by Agent, or by Attorney

The board of adjustment shall fix a reasonable time for the hearing of the appeal, give public notice thereof, as well as due notice to the parties in interest, and decide the same within a reasonable time. Upon the hearing, any party may appear in person or by agent or by attorney.

(On the matter of notice and hearing, the strict constructionist will find that under the Standard Act public notice and hearing are required only on appeals from decisions of the administrative official and *not* on special exceptions or variances. This is probably an unintentional omission remedied in states where more positive action has not been taken by ignoring it. It is now standard practice to require public notice and hearing on all three major board functions.)

State enabling acts contain variations on this wording, sometimes detailing the type and timing of notice required. More specific requirements are also included in local ordinance or board rules.

Vote Required to Reverse Official or Decide in Favor of Applicant

The concurring vote of four members of the board shall be necessary to reverse any order, requirement, decision, or determination of any such administrative officials, or to decide in favor of the applicant on any matter upon which it is required to pass under any such ordinance, or to effect any variation in such ordinance.

State variations from this Standard Act language are common. Virginia, for example, requires the concurring vote of a majority of the board members.[4] Georgia, with boards consisting of not less than three nor more than five members, makes no requirement for an extraordinary majority.[5] In California, enabling legislation allows for a broad range of devices for performing usual board functions, but does not specify size of boards of adjustment and makes no mention of any extraordinary majority.[6]

Where not covered by state statute or the zoning ordinance, board rules should be specific as to the number of concurring votes needed (certainly not less than a majority of the entire board), and a quorum should obviously consist of at least that number.

An Introduction to the Checklist

Table 1 is a checklist of matters relating to the board which need coverage *someplace* in the maze of state statutes, local ordinances, or rules. Pecking order is one element in sorting things out. The generality-specificity spectrum is another. Determinations on local public policy of substantial importance should probably be handled by ordinance rather than board rules.

The pecking order (below the federal level) begins with any state acts generally affecting boards and board members and the state zoning enabling act. (Matters are complicated enough without going into home rule or charter provisions laying out a smorgasbord of supplemental and/or substitute powers, procedures, limitations, or requirements, but these will need to be considered in localities where they apply.)

Second come local ordinances, legally required to be in accord with state law. Third are rules of the board, legally required to be in accord with both state law and local ordinances.

Comes now the generality-specificity spectrum. On many matters, zoning enabling legislation is broad-brush, stating general requirements or giving general powers. The local jurisdiction may or may not provide for special exceptions, but if it does the board is bound in its decisions by the terms of the local ordinance. If the ordinance provides for a particular special exception by name only, with no guides or standards for judgment, the latitude for board action is increased to the point where arbitrary and capricious decisions become a strong possibility.

"The board shall adopt rules *in accordance with the provisions of any ordinance adopted* pursuant to this act," says the Standard Act. Here again, where the ordinance omits important details, the board is left to its own devices and may go astray.

"The board of adjustment shall fix a reasonable time for the hearing of the appeal, give public notice thereof, as well as due notice to the parties in interest, and decide the same within a reasonable time." Unless state zoning enabling acts have added more precise language on these points (and many have, particularly on the matter of public notice), it is left to the locality to add specificity. What is a "reasonable time" from application to hearing, what form should public notice and due notice to parties in interest take, and how long should be allowed between the hearing and the decision?

Without the intervention of ordinance language, determination is left to the board and should be reflected in its rules (although nothing in the

TABLE 1

State and Local Sources on Organization, Powers, Requirements, and Procedures

Boards of Adjustment

Subject	State Acts[1]		Local[2] Ordinances		Board Rules
	General	Zoning	General	Zoning	
1. General provisions					
1.1. State and local statutes, board rules applicable	X	X	X	X	X
1.2. Requirement for familiarity with above	—	—	—	—	X
1.3. Current form of rules to be available to public	—	—	—	—	X
1.4. Location of board offices	—	—	—	—	X
2. Members (and alternates if permitted)					
2.1. Number	—	X	—	X	—
2.2. Qualifications	—	—	—	X	—
2.3. Appointment, appointing body	—	X	—	—	—
2.4. Terms	—	X	—	X	—
2.5. Compensation	—	—	—	X	—
2.6. Removable for cause by appointing authority	—	X	—	X	—
2.6.1. Procedures—written charges, public hearing	—	X	—	X	—
2.6.2. Causes for removal specified	—	—	—	X	X
2.7. Vacancies (other than in cases of removal; notification of appointing authority	—	—	—	—	X
2.7.1. Filling vacancies; term	—	X	—	—	—
3. Officers and duties; staff and duties					
3.1. Manner of selection of officers (chairman; acting or vice-chairman	—	—	—	X	X
3.2. Chairman or acting chairman may administer oaths, compel attendance of witnesses	—	X	—	—	—
3.3. Terms; limitations on succession if any	—	—	—	X	—
3.4. Secretary, manner of selection, qualifications	—	X	—	X	—
3.4.1. Keeping of minutes and records (to be public records, filed in office of board)	—	—	—	X	—
3.5. Provision for other staff assistance	—	—	—	—	—

	1	2	3	4	5
4. Committees of the board, appointment					
4.1. Standing committees	—	—	—	—	×
4.2. Other committees	—	—	—	—	×
5. Rules of procedure: adoption, amendment, waiving, or suspending					
5.1. To be adopted	—	×	—	—	—
5.2. Amendment of rules	—	—	—	—	—
5.2.1. Notice to board members	—	—	—	×	—
5.2.2. Majority vote of all members required	—	—	—	×	—
5.3. Waiving or suspending rules	—	—	—	×	—
5.3.1. Limitations	—	—	—	×	—
5.3.2. Majority vote of quorum present required	—	—	—	×	—
6. Conduct of members					
6.1. Not to represent applicants or appellants before board	—	—	—	×	—
6.2. Limitations on conflict of interest	—	×	—	—	—
6.3. "Sunshine law" limitations	—	×	—	—	—
6.4. Not to discuss pending cases with applicants or appellants, or express opinions on merits, except as part of official proceedings	—	—	—	×	—
7. Appeals and applications: notice of public hearings; amendment of applications or appeals; deferrals; withdrawals					
7.1. Appeals from decisions of administrative officer	—	—	—	×	—
7.1.1. Time limitations	—	×	—	—	×
7.1.2. Where and how filed	—	×	—	—	—
7.1.3. Action of official appealed from	—	×	—	—	—
7.1.4. Appeal stays proceedings in furtherance of action appealed from, except in cases of imminent peril to life or property	—	×	—	—	—

Continued on next page

1. Only Standard Act provisions are included in this summary. Check applicable state statutes.

2. In some jurisdictions, the local ordinance establishing the board and covering most of the details of its operation is separate from the zoning ordinance, which covers only matters to be referred to it.

TABLE 1

Continued

Subject	State Acts[1]		Local[2] Ordinances		Board Rules
	General	Zoning	General	Zoning	
7.2. Applications for special exceptions, appeals for variances; where and how filed	—	—	—	X	—
7.3. Time limits between filing and public hearing	—	—	—	X	X
7.4. Actions between time of filing and public hearing	—	—	—	—	X
7.4.1. Assigning case number	—	—	—	—	X
(7.4.2. Preliminary conference with applicants)	—	—	—	—	(X)
7.4.3. Scheduling hearing	—	—	—	—	X
7.4.4. Notice of hearing	—	X	—	X	X
7.4.5. Amendment of applications or appeals; deferrals; withdrawals prior to public hearing	—	—	—	—	X
8. Meetings, hearings					
8.1. Regular meetings, time and place	—	X[3]	—	—	X
8.1.1. Cancellation	—	—	—	—	X
8.1.2. Change in time or place	—	—	—	—	X
8.2. Special meetings	—	—	—	—	X
8.2.1. How called, notice to board members, other notice	—	—	—	—	X
8.2.2. Cancellation	—	—	—	—	X
8.2.3. Change in time or place	—	—	—	—	X
8.3. Adjourned meetings	—	—	—	—	X
8.4. Quorums	—	X[4]	—	—	X
8.5. All meetings to be public	—	X	—	—	X
8.6. Records required	—	X	—	—	—
8.6.1. Matter to be recorded	—	X	—	—	X
8.6.2. Records to be public, filed in office of board	—	—	—	—	X
8.7. Order of business at meetings	—	—	—	—	X
8.7.1. Regular or special meetings, without public hearings or prior to public hearings	—	—	—	—	X

	1	2	3	4	5
8.7.2. Public hearings required	—	—	—	×	—
8.7.2.1. Who may appear	—	×[5]	—	—	×
8.7.2.2. Order of business generally	—	×	—	—	×
8.7.2.3. Order of hearing of cases	—	—	—	—	—
8.7.2.4. Procedure where board members are disqualified by conflict of interest or for other reasons	—	—	×	×	×
8.7.2.5. Requests to amend appeals or applications	—	—	—	—	×
8.7.2.6. Requests for deferral or continuance of hearings	—	—	—	—	×
8.7.2.7. Requests for withdrawal of appeals or applications	—	—	—	—	×
8.8. Rehearings; reconsideration of cases	—	—	—	—	×
8.9. Character of hearings; disruption prohibited	—	—	×	—	×
9. Matters to be considered at hearings to support findings and decisions					
9.1. Appeals from decisions of administrative official	—	×[6]	—	—	—
9.2. Applications for special exceptions	—	×[6]	—	×	—
9.3. Appeals for variances	—	×	—	—	×
10. Findings and decisions					
10.1. Written findings required	—	×[6]	—	×	×
10.2. Time limits for decisions	—	×	—	×	—
10.3. Attaching conditions and safeguards	—	×[6]	—	×	×
10.4. Notifying applicants or appellants	—	×	—	×	×
11. Appeals from decisions of board of adjustment					
11.1. Time limit	—	×	—	—	—

3. "Meetings . . . shall be held at the call of the chairman and at such other times as the board may determine."

4. Standard Act requires vote of four out of five members to reverse administrative official or decide in favor of applicant. For these purposes a quorum would thus be four, unless absent members are authorized to vote after reading record, a generally undesirable arrangement.

5. Careful reading of the Standard Act indicates that it requires notice and hearing only on appeals from decisions of administrative officials and not on special exceptions and variances. In practice, notice and hearing are generally required on all three actions.

6. Standard Act provisions are general and in some cases partial here. The local ordinance often adds specificity which board rules must respect, since its rules "must be in accordance with the provisions of any ordinance adopted pursuant to this act."

Standard Act *requires* this kind of coverage). Where state legislation lacks further instruction, ordinances of most jurisdictions include provisions covering some or all of the issues.

On determining policy by legislative action rather than board rules, the example above serves as a beginning. Does the governing body feel that it is of substantial importance to establish time limits for board action and the manner and timing of notice, or is it willing to leave these details to the board itself?

The variance issue provides another example. Standard Act language (except as it has been modified in many states) establishes these cumulative requirements relating to variances:

1. The variance will not be contrary to the public interest.

2. There are special conditions.

3. Literal enforcement of the terms of the ordinance will result in unnecessary hardship.

4. The spirit of the ordinance shall be observed and substantial justice done.

These are generalities affecting matters of substantial public importance. Unless the ordinance adds specificity, the board has no further guidance. It seems entirely appropriate for the legislative body to indicate types of potential variances which would *not* be in accord with the spirit of the ordinance (such as use variances), to define and describe the public interest (particularly in intent statements applying generally or relating to specific districts), to indicate what types of special conditions must be involved, and to identify the kind of unnecessary hardship justifying a variance. (The position of the legislative body would be reenforced in such definitions and limitations if guided by prevailing court interpretations. Some of the guidelines suggested above appear beginning at page 31.)

As a final example of pecking order, generality versus specificity, and ordinance language versus board rules, there is the matter of removal of board members "for cause by the appointing authority upon written charges and after public hearing." Here specificity in board rules would be helpful as a guide to members, perhaps in more exact terms than mal-, mis-, or non-feasance or cantankerous ineptitude, with violation of board rules specifically listed in the ordinance as cause for removal, since the appointing authority will usually be the governing body. Table 1 traces major permutations.

Variations on Detailed Board Rules

No model rules can apply universally to boards across the country.
Excerpts from Standard Act language and sample modifications from
various states as discussed above are one reason. For another, there is
the complexity of subject matter and possibilities of having it appear in
several places and in varying degrees of detail.

**Rules governing board action extend far beyond rules adopted by the
board for its own governance.** This establishes a choice as to how rules
of the board should be structured. In their simplest form, they might be
merely supplemental, as required for parliamentary guidance, adopting
Roberts' Rules of Order with such modifications and additions as seem
appropriate, setting dates and places for meetings (if this has not already
been done in the zoning ordinance), and handling other "housekeeping"
details. In this case, the board rules leave members uninstructed on many
things they need to know if they are to operate effectively. As a supple-
ment to such rules, there might be a list of cross-references to sources for
other guidance. Unless such sources are obtained and read, board
members will still remain uninformed.

At the other extreme, there may be board rules which not only cover
"housekeeping" detail, but go on to incorporate all applicable detailed
language from state and local ordinance sources. Here members may
operate with full and coordinated guidance before them. But there are
disadvantages in the full-scale approach, too, unless it is very carefully
handled. Without full footnoting, members may not be clear as to which
rules their body may waive or amend. And amendments to state legislation or local ordinances (unless noted and reflected promptly in board
rules) may put the board out of step with current limitations or
requirements.

Usually it is best to compromise between these poles. The board, and
preferably each of its members, should have a kit containing: (a) the
board's own rules concerning conduct of its own internal affairs; (b) pertinent material from state enabling legislation or general legislation affecting operation of boards and conduct of public officials; (c) the zoning ordinance and other applicable general laws or excerpts affecting the
board; and (d) a tabular index along the lines of Table 1, indicating location of subject matter and how it is related.

As a further source of guidance, state planning associations, state planning agencies, and universities often publish manuals, compilations of
planning and zoning legislation, and reports on judicial activity. National

sources, such as the American Planning Association, also have helpful information. The board should maintain a library of such material for guidance in its operations. (Obviously, it would be most desirable to have competent legal advice in assembling and interpreting the kit, drafting board rules, and continuing maintenance and updating operations.)

In what follows, organization and language for board rules is suggested, sometimes with a choice among variations. In some instances, wording for inclusion in the zoning ordinance is indicated for use where state legislation does not cover points in adequate detail.

Material is arranged in the same general order as in Table 1, but numbering of sections and subsections varies from that in the table because of added detail.

General Statutes, Ordinances, and Rules Applying to the Board

Article 1. General Governing Statutes, Ordinances, and Rules
The board of adjustment, hereinafter referred to as "the board," shall be governed by all of the following statutes, ordinances, and rules:

  1.1.   *Applicable State Statutes and Local Ordinances and Rules.*

To the extent that they remain in force and effect, as they are amended, or as they may be added to, the board and its members and officers shall be governed by state statutes and local ordinances including the following:

  a. *State statutes applying generally to public boards, members, and officials,* including:

    (Here list applicable statutes on conflict of interest, "sunshine" laws, and the like.)

  b. *State statutes relating to activities of boards of adjustment in relation to planning and zoning,* including:

    (Here list applicable planning and zoning enabling acts, particularly identifying portions related to activities of boards.)

  c. *Ordinances and rules of (jurisdiction) generally affecting its local boards and officials,* including:

    (List general ordinances and rules of the character indicated.)

  d. *The zoning ordinance of (jurisdiction).*

  e. *The rules of the board,* as set forth herein.

  1.2.   *Requirement for Familiarity with State Statutes and Local Ordinances and Rules Affecting the Board.*

Upon taking office, all members of the board shall familiarize themselves with the foregoing, and, while in office, members shall maintain such knowledge, including knowledge of amendments and additions, and shall be strictly governed thereby in the conduct of board affairs.

Language along the lines of 1.2 above is not common, but it should be. It is not too much to ask that board members know what they are doing, and under what limitations. Violation of this rule, under the arrangement indicated on page 65, might be grounds for cause for removal of members who persist in ignorance or feel that their interpretation of justice transcends mere law.

1.3. *Rules of Board to Be Available to Public in Board Office.*

A certified official copy of rules of the board, in current form, shall be available in the office of the board as a public record. Additional copies shall be provided to members of the board and made available to the public on request, but the official copy in the board's office shall govern. No amendment to these rules shall become effective until incorporated in the official copy.

This provision could go into the ordinance in addition to, or instead of, the rules. It parallels common requirements on the official zoning map, assuring that those who wish to know can find out about board rules, and that there will be no rules in effect which are not in the official public record. If the board does not have a regular office, another appropriate source should be specified.

1.4. *Location of Board Office.*

The office of the board shall be at _____.

Here again, the provision might appear in the ordinance. If in the rules, it might be expanded to indicate days and hours when the office is normally open, particularly if operations are to be part-time. Placing operational details directly in the ordinance makes changes awkward because of amendment requirements.

Provisions Relating to Members

State law generally covers number of members (and alternates, if permitted), appointment, terms, removal for cause (stated generally), and the filling of vacancies. Taking these in order (as related to the statute-ordinance-rules division) and filling in gaps, if there is latitude as to number or terms of members or alternates, the matter should be settled in the ordinance, which might also establish qualifications for membership.

Qualifications for membership vary. There may be only a simple statement requiring members to be residents of the jurisdiction. There may also be a prohibition against members holding elected or appointed office in the jurisdiction (and sometimes in other jurisdictions) with an exception to allow a member of the planning commission to serve for liaison purposes.

There might well be a performance-related standard along these lines:

> No member shall be appointed to or remain on the board whose business, profession, activities, property holdings, or personal relationships are such as to create the probability of frequent disqualification from voting on ground of conflict of interest.

On compensation of members, most ordinances are silent or indicate that they shall serve without compensation. Some provide for compensation, usually with a fixed amount per meeting and sometimes with a maximum amount per year. (One ordinance sets the meeting fee at $25 and $600 as the annual maximum. In the jurisdiction involved, the number of regular and special meetings held tends to correspond more closely with limitations set by the maximum figure than with public requirements.) Occasionally, there is stated allowance for mileage and other expenses incidental to board business.

The *manner* of removal for cause by the appointing body (usually the governing body) might well be spelled out in the ordinance unless general laws or regulations apply. Items to be considered are specificity of written charges, requirements for notice of the hearing to the member and the public, whether an extraordinary majority is required to remove, and the form of the action.

Causes for removal might also be detailed in the ordinance (and perhaps repeated in board rules), or could be stated only in the rules. If rules can be amended by the board without agreement by the governing body, placement of these elements in the ordinance is indicated. Some causes are listed in illustrative language at Section 2.2, below.

Vacancies are to be filled for the unexpired term, according to usual state law, but there is no indication as to how vacancies are created. By death, certainly, or by resignation. But there are a number of other contingencies to be considered, and these probably belong in the rules, with language along the lines of Sections 2.3 and 2.4, below.

Another gap in many state zoning enabling statutes involves unfilled vacancies. Without remedial ordinance provisions, board operations may be suspended or hampered because of delays by the appointing body in finding and appointing members to succeed. The cure here is usually language continuing members in office until their successors are appointed, with any appropriate limitations. The Tucson ordinance, for example, states:

> The term of each member shall be for one year. However, unless a successor is appointed within 60 days of each subsequent anniversary date of a member's appointment to the board, the term of the member shall be extended for one year.[7]

Article 2. Members

2.1. *Number of Members and Alternates; Appointment; Qualifications; Terms; Compensation; Procedure for Removal; Procedure for Filling Vacancies; and Terms of Members Appointed to Fill Vacancies.*

Number of members and alternates; appointment; qualifications; terms; compensation; procedure for removal; procedure for filling vacancies; and terms of members appointed to fill vacancies shall be as provided in *(indicate sections of ordinance).*

2.2. *Causes for Removal from Board.*

Causes for removal of members (including alternates) from the board by the *(appointing body)* shall include malfeasance, misfeasance, or nonfeasance generally, and in particular:

a. Failure to maintain reasonable familiarity with state statutes and local ordinances and rules affecting the board, or failure to be governed thereby, as required by Section 1.2, above.

b. Failure to disclose conflict of interest for purposes of disqualification when a member has personal or monetary interest in the matter involved, or will be directly affected by a decision of the board.

If conflict of interest is covered and/or otherwise defined in a state statute or local ordinance, language here should correspond and/or there should be a reference to the source.

2.3. *Resignations, Generally, and by Absence.*

When members propose to resign, if reasonably feasible, they shall give notice of their intent to the chairman or secretary, or make the date of resignation effective, in such a manner as to allow time for appointment of replacements.

Failure to attend three consecutive regular meetings, or three of any seven consecutive meetings, without the recorded consent of the chairman, shall be construed as resignation from the board by absence. This provision shall apply to regular members and to alternates when requested to serve in the place of regular members.

2.4. *Vacation of Office.*

When a member dies or resigns (including resignation by absence), the secretary shall promptly indicate to the _(appointing body)_ that a vacancy exists. When a member becomes incapacitated for office permanently or for what appears likely to be a protracted period, or moves from the jurisdiction, or becomes for any other reason no longer qualified for office, and fails to resign, the chairman shall cause any necessary investigation to be made and if appropriate shall declare the office vacant, and the secretary shall promptly indicate to the _(appointing body)_ that a vacancy exists.

In many jurisdictions, vacancies and absences cause problems and result in inequitable treatment or delays, particularly if there is no provision for the use of alternate members. Where an applicant or appellant appears before four members of a five-member board, and four votes are necessary to favor his cause, he must convince 100 percent of the members present, rather than 80 percent. With a five-member board, absence of two members or a two-member vacancy paralyzes the board for lack of a quorum (again assuming that alternates are not authorized).

Thus it is very important, in the ordinance or board rules, to provide for foreseeing vacancies as early as possible, for declaring vacancies with a minimum of delay, and for notifying the appointing body promptly.

Language suggested at Sections 2.3 and 2.4 has this purpose. The first paragraph of 2.3, with its "where reasonably feasible" escape hatch, is more of a reminder than a mandate. The second paragraph, with its provision for "automatic resignation," provides an alternate to the more lengthy and involved procedure for removal for nonfeasance (which might still be used in obstinate cases). "Without the recorded consent of the chairman," although it weakens the effect, allows for exercise of discretion.

The final paragraph of Section 2.4 deals with a variety of possibilities. A member moves from the jurisdiction and fails to resign or to notify the secretary. Is the move temporary or permanent? If permanent, it should be possible to vacate his office without waiting for him to miss three consecutive meetings. A member is elected to an office and fails to resign in a jurisdiction prohibiting holding of more than one elective or appointive office. A member is reported to have an incurable and incapacitating disease and is unable to resign because of his condition.

In such cases, it should not be necessary to invoke removal proceedings. Where necessary, the chairman should have the circumstances investigated, but, when there is clearly a vacancy, it should be possible to proceed to fill it with a minimum of red tape and delay. As a safeguard, some jurisdictions may require action by the board or even the governing body, but this might well be reserved for cases where there is a shadow of doubt as to whether the vacancy exists.

Officers, Committees, Staff, Duties

Here again, state statutes and local ordinances should be examined for variations both in themselves and in the amount of flexibility left for rules. On the matter of officers, for example, the chairman of the board may be appointed by the governing body or its presiding officer, rather than elected by the board. There may be limitations on succession in office. Relation between time of election and time of taking office may vary, as in cases where officers take their new posts at the end of the meeting in which elected or the beginning of the next, to allow for a smoother transition.

Availability of staff is another variable. Depending on local circumstances and personnel resources, staff may vary from none, with a member serving as secretary, to a staff with several members. Often the zoning administrator is also secretary of the board. A member of the planning department staff may be assigned to serve full or part time, and the planning department may be made responsible for preparing reports and recommendations in all cases or in certain classes of cases. In large jurisdictions, the board may have its own attorney. In others, it should obviously have access to legal counsel serving the jurisdiction generally.

Article 3. Officers, Committees, Staff, Duties

3.1. *Regular Election of Chairman, Vice-Chairman; Provisions for Contingencies; Continuation of Service Until Successors Take Office.*

Annually, as the last item of new business at the regular meeting of the board in the month of _____, the board shall elect a chairman and vice-chairman. If such regular meeting is cancelled or a quorum is lacking, the election shall be held within 36 days thereafter at a regular or special meeting. If no quorum can be obtained within 36 days, the election shall be held at a regular or special meeting held as soon thereafter as a quorum can be obtained, provided that if no such election is held within 60 days of the date when generally required, the secretary shall notify the (*governing body*), which shall appoint a chairman and vice-chairman to serve until the next regular election in the month of _____. The prior chairman and acting chairman shall remain in office until their successors take office at the next regular or special meeting following their election or appointment.

3.1.1. *Succession of Vice-Chairman to Office of Chairman; Special Elections.*

If the chairman resigns his office or becomes no longer a member of the board, the vice-chairman shall succeed him in office for the remainder of the term. If the vice-chairman resigns his office, becomes no longer a member of the board, or succeeds to the chairman's office, a special election shall be held at the next regular meeting of the board to select a vice-chairman to complete the term, provided that if such regular meeting is one immediately preceding the regular election and any duties to be performed by the vice-chairman in the intervening period can be performed in a satisfactory manner, the board may permit the office of vice-chairman to remain vacant for the period.

The first set of provisions above covers a number of contingencies, including the possibility that the governing body may have to step in. (This provision should of course be used only if state statutes and the ordinance allow sufficient leeway.) The second set plugs what is often a hole in board rules, the matter of a special election to fill a vacancy in the office of vice-chairman. Rules *could* require a special election to fill the chairman's post if vacated, but those above conform to normal practice.

3.2. *Duties of Chairman and Vice-Chairman; Appointment of Temporary Chairman to Preside at Meetings.*

3.2.1. *Presiding at Meetings.*

If present and able, the chairman shall preside at all meetings and hearings. If the chairman is absent or unable to preside, the vice-chairman shall preside. If both are absent or unable to preside, the members present shall appoint a temporary chairman to preside.

In accordance with these and other applicable rules, the presiding officer shall decide all points of procedure or order, unless otherwise directed by a majority of the members in attendance on motion duly made and passed. He shall maintain order and decorum, and to that end may order removal of disorderly or disruptive persons. He shall administer oaths to all witnesses, or arrange for such oaths to be administered.

Again, foreseeable contingencies are covered. "Unable to preside" covers laryngitis and other physical disabilities, but also possible disqualification in a particular case. Language on appointment of a temporary chairman should of course be used only where the board has enough members and/or alternates so that absence of both chairman and vice-chairman leaves a quorum for transaction of such business as may be on hand.

The charge to maintain order and decorum is made explicit, giving the presiding officer something to read aloud to dampen incipient riots.

On the matter of swearing witnesses, some rules leave this optional: "the chairman *may* administer oaths and compel the attendance of witnesses," says the Standard Act, and the language is carried forward into the rules unchanged. Selective swearing of witnesses implies that some are felt more likely to lie than others. This gives offense and could lead to legal problems. If some witnesses are to be sworn, all should be sworn. The equality of treatment should extend to staff witnesses, who can usually be sworn once generally, with the matter confirmed in future appearances.

3.2.2. Other Responsibilities and Duties of Chairman; Delegation to Vice-Chairman.

The chairman shall have further duties and responsibilities, as indicated below. He may delegate specific duties generally to the vice-chairman or may authorize the vice-chairman to perform specific duties, during his absence from the jurisdiction or in case of his other disability to perform necessary board functions in a timely manner. The vice-chairman shall perform all duties so delegated, and in case of absence or incapacity of the chairman, on approval by majority of the board, shall perform any or all duties of the chairman whether or not delegated.

This section charges the chairman with the listed duties and responsibilities, but allows him to decide which to delegate or for how long. He may delegate part of his duties generally (as, for example, making or supervising preparation of reports to the governing body). He may reserve on such matters as committee appointments in his absence. The final sentence is a fail-safe provision covering emergencies where the chairman is absent or incapacitated and has not made specific delegation. In this case, the approval of the majority of the board is in lieu of delegation by the chairman.

The chairman and vice-chairman usually have other duties. Most rules (where such other duties are mentioned at all) lay the responsibilities on the chairman, with the assumption that he can delegate any or all of them or that in his absence the vice-chairman may perform any or all of them.

Under such an arrangement, the following illustration demonstrates a problem that may develop. The chairman is away for a month. There has been discussion of establishing a committee that will have important duties, but there is nothing immediately pressing about it. The chairman and vice-chairman have strongly divergent views on some matters. In the absence of the chairman, the vice-chairman proceeds on the business of setting up the committee and himself appoints members more likely to share his views than those of the chairman.

There is a question of local policy here. How strong is the chairman's position intended to be? Wording below assumes a strong chairman, but gives the board power to override his decisions on certain matters.

3.2.2.1. Managerial Responsibilities.

Subject to these rules and further instructions from the board, the chairman shall direct the official business of the board, supervise the work of the secretary as it relates to the affairs of the board, request needed assistance, direct the work of the staff, and exercise general disciplinary power.

Section 3.2.2.1, virtually verbatim from the Tucson ordinance cited, establishes the managerial responsibilities of the chairman. Most rules leave management floating in midair. These seem to be a desirable improvement. Somebody should run the show, and basic responsibility should be stated in the rules.

3.2.2.2. *Assignment of Board Members to Inspection Duties; Assignment of Alternates to Board Duty; Appointment of Committees.*

The chairman may designate members of the board to make personal inspections when necessary for the proper consideration of cases; shall assign alternates to serve in the absence or disability of regular board members; and shall appoint such committees as may be found necessary.

Section 3.2.2.2 as stated assumes that inspections by some of the board members, at least, are local practice in more important cases (rather than depending entirely on reports by staff or the presentations by applicants or appellants—or opponents—at public hearings). The chairman is given carte blanche as to which members will be selected. As an alternative, rules might specify that members be assigned review duties in turn, as nearly as feasible and convenient. The section also assumes that there are alternates, which will certainly not be true in all jurisdictions (in the case of Tucson, for example, with a seven-member board and a quorum of four, alternates are not felt necessary). Specific provision might be made in the rules for service of alternates on a rotating basis, as nearly as feasible and convenient. As stated, it is assumed that the chairman will appoint on this basis.

3.2.2.3. *Reporting to the Board; for the Board.*

The chairman shall report to the board on all official transactions which have not otherwise come to the attention of the board. The chairman shall also make or cause to be made any reports concerning the affairs of the board required or requested by the _____[8].

At Section 3.2.2.3, the chairman is given basic responsibility for reporting to the board on official matters that might not otherwise come to their attention. More important, perhaps, is reporting "as required or requested" to the governing body. Many ordinances require an annual report on board affairs, and governing bodies should be informed at least occasionally on board activities.

Warning Signals
Too great a case load on variances, with most of them granted, indicates
a "runaway" board abusing its powers. A high case load on appeals from
decisions of the administrative official is a red flag. The ordinance
probably needs clarifying revision. A high case load on special exceptions means that the board is overloaded with duties in this category.
Other special permitting procedures should be used for classes of cases
with the least potential impact on neighborhoods or neighboring
property.

3.3. *Appointment of Secretary; Duties.*

3.3.1. *Appointment.*

The secretary to the board shall be appointed by _____ and shall
be _____.

Because of variations in local practice and personnel resources, illustrative language here must be mostly blanks. If the secretary is to be
a member of the board or is to be solely an employee of the board, appointment should be by the board. If the secretary is the zoning administrator, his deputy or agent, or another member of the building
department staff, or a member of the planning staff assigned full or part
time to the secretarial duties involved, this might better be settled by the
ordinance than the rules. If determination is in the rules, the blanks above
should contain language like "city manager" or "county executive" for
the first, and "member of the building department (or planning department) staff" for the second.

To have the *board* appoint a member of the planning or building staff
to serve as its secretary complicates lines of administrative responsibility. (On supervision, the problem of having a member of the planning
or building department staff serve two masters is limited by charging the
chairman with supervising the work of the secretary only "as it relates
to the affairs of the board."

3.3.2. *Duties of the Secretary.*

Subject to the provisions of the zoning ordinance, these rules, and the direction of the board and its chairman, the secretary shall in general attend to
all correspondence of the board; send out or cause to be published all notices
required; attend all meetings of the board and all hearings (except when excused by the chairman of the board and with temporary services arranged);
scrutinize all matters to assure compliance with the zoning ordinance and
these rules; compile all required records; maintain the necessary schedules,
files, and indexes; and generally perform or supervise all clerical work of
the board. In particular:

3.3.2.1. *Docket Book.*

The secretary shall maintain a docket book which shall be kept posted to date. The secretary shall enter in the docket book the number of the case, the name of the applicant, the location of the premises by street number or otherwise, the nature of the case, and, when completed, the final disposition. All continuances, postponements, dates of sending notes, and other steps taken and acts done shall be noted on the docket.

3.3.2.2. *Minute Book; Minutes a Public Record.*

The secretary shall maintain a minute book which shall be kept posted to date. In the minute book shall be recorded the board's proceedings, showing attendance and all absences, with indications as to whether absences were excused or unexcused by the chairman, any disqualifications of members, the record of its examinations and all other official actions, and the vote of each member voting on every question.[9] The minutes of the board shall be a public record, kept in the offices of the board.

3.3.2.3. *Notification of Expiration of Terms of Members; Vacancies.*

At least 60 days prior to expiration of terms of members, and as promptly as feasible where a member resigns with a deferred effective date or when a member's office is vacated, as provided at Section 2.4, the secretary shall notify the _____ that a vacancy exists and request the appointment of a successor.

The final subsection above is another device to keep membership as nearly at full strength as possible. In jurisdictions where terms are for more than one year and there is overlapping, the secretary should also indicate the length of the term to be filled.

Other Staff or Committee Assistance—Variations

Board rules or other staff or committee assistance must be tailored to fit staff available to the board directly or in other agencies, and duties prescribed by the zoning ordinance, general law, or local policy. The zoning administrator may be secretary of the board, with no other help available. There may be a secretary in addition to the zoning administrator. In the absence of adequate staff, committees of the board may be assigned to certain duties.

In some jurisdictions, matters to come before the board are first referred to the planning department or commission for study and report, and some planning departments have staff members assigned full or part time to zoning matters (including proposals for amendments as well as reports on appeals or applications). Detailed requirements on this kind of referral belong in the zoning ordinance, but the manner of processing should be reflected in board rules to relate time requirements to scheduling of notice and hearings.

Under Variation I below, the zoning administrator is not also secretary of the board:

Variation I

3.4. Duties of Zoning Administrator.

The zoning administrator, or his authorized deputies or assistants, shall have the following duties and responsibilities in relation to appeals and applications. He shall receive all appeals and applications and examine the material submitted therewith to assure that it is complete and that required maps, plans, or reports are in good order, and in sufficient number for processing and recording. He shall transmit the originals of such documents to the secretary of the board for docketing, placing on the calendar, and preparation and publication of public notice of the hearing. As appropriate to the nature of the case, he shall make or cause to be made an inspection of the premises, and be prepared to advise the board of conditions on the property and relation to other properties likely to be affected.

State law generally requires appeals to be filed with the officer from whom the appeal is taken (when on grounds of alleged administrative error). It is also usual practice to make the zoning administrator responsible for receipt of applications for special exceptions and appeals for variances. Common sense dictates that, on filing, the official should check material for completeness and accuracy.

On inspection of the premises and reporting to the board, there may be considerable variation. The board as a whole may make the inspection, a very commendable practice in important cases. A committee of the board may be appointed for such purposes, perhaps with other duties as outlined in Variation II below. Or the duty may be assigned to the planning department, as indicated in Variation III.

Variation II. Committee for Preliminary Review

Rules above charge the chairman with the duty of appointing necessary committees. This may be all the rules need say about committees. In some cases, however, it may be a good idea to provide for specific committees and to establish duties and requirements.

Particularly in smaller jurisdictions where staff is limited, committees for preliminary review may perform functions which might otherwise be handled by staff, viewing premises and reporting the situation to the full board. If this is all such a committee does, there may be no need for formal identification in the rules.

An additional function which might be performed involves prehearing conferences with applicants or appellants. In such cases, on request, the committee meets with the applicant or appellant to explore the case in greater detail (and under less stress) than might be possible at the hearing, to sift and organize information (and determine whether more is needed in a particular case), and to explain points which the applicant or appellant may not fully understand. If well handled, such procedure streamlines and improves the conduct of hearings.

Given this function, rules should be specific. The purpose of the operation is to assist in preparing for proper presentation of the case, not deciding it. This should be made clear to both committee members and applicants. Meetings with the committee should conform strictly to any "sunshine" laws. It would be well to specify the meeting place and date for such meetings in the rules, and to require posting notice in the office of the board. The meeting should be open. Considering its purpose, the public is not invited, but neither is it barred. It is emphasized again that the committee function here is to assist in preparing the case, not to argue it.

A permutation on this approach might run as follows:

3.4   Duties of Zoning Administrator.

The zoning administrator, or his authorized deputies or assistants, shall have the following duties and responsibilities in relation to appeals and applications. He shall receive all appeals and applications and examine the material submitted therewith to assure that it is complete and that required maps, plans, or reports are in good order and in sufficient number for processing and recording. He shall notify applicants or appellants of the function of the committee for preliminary review, and the time and place of the next regular meeting of the committee at which a review could be scheduled, and shall determine whether an appearance before the committee is requested. He shall transmit the originals of appeals and applications and materials submitted therewith to the secretary of the board for docketing, placing on the calendar, and preparation and publication of public notice of the hearing, and shall notify the secretary of any application to appear before the committee for preliminary review.

Here the zoning administrator is charged with two duties concerning the committee for preliminary review. He must notify the applicant or appellant as to its function and pass the word to the secretary of the board if a meeting with the committee is requested. If this approach is followed, the provisions concerning the duties of the secretary might be enlarged to include posting, in the board office, of the names of appellants or applicants to meet with the committee, the committee members serving, and the matter being considered.

Variation III. Planning Department to Inspect Premises and Report

Where the planning department is charged with duties relating to board activities, language might run as follows:

3.4 *Duties of Zoning Administrator and of Planning Department.*

The zoning administrator, or his authorized deputies or assistants, shall have the following duties and responsibilities in relation to appeals and applications. He shall receive all appeals and applications and examine the material submitted therewith to assure that it is complete and that required maps, plans, or reports to be submitted by applicants or appellants are in good order and in sufficient number for processing and recording.

He shall transmit one copy of such documents to the planning department for its review, report on inspection of premises and recommendations, and the planning department shall, within 10 days (or such longer period as may be agreed to in particular cases by the secretary of the board), review the appeal or application, make inspection of the premises, and prepare its report or recommendation.

The original application or appeal and other documents submitted shall be transmitted to the secretary of the board for docketing, placing on the calendar, and preparation and publication of public notice of the hearing, together with such other notice as is appropriate in the particular case.

As to administrative mechanics here, the administrator transmits the original to the secretary and a copy to the planning department at the same time. Under the 10-day rule (as extended in particularly complicated cases), the secretary is then prepared to set things in motion for the hearing.

Wording above is left flexible as to presentation of the planning department report. It is to be *prepared* within 10 days. This allows for a brief written summary and an oral presentation in some cases, or longer documentation in other.

3.5 *Duties of Legal Counsel.*

The (*jurisdictional attorney or department of law*) shall provide legal advice to the board as to matters under its jurisdiction and may assist in interrogating witnesses. Advice of counsel shall be received and entered in the minutes before disposition of any question of law or matter requiring legal interpretation or advice.

The board should have legal advice and assistance. In most places, it will not have its own attorney, but is given access to the legal department or attorney for the jurisdiction. The Tucson *Rules*, from which this language is derived, are commendable both in giving access to counsel and in calling for legal advice on questions of law or matters requiring legal interpretation before the board makes its decision.

Conduct of Board Members, Staff

Limitations on conduct may appear in general state legislation, zoning enabling legislation, local ordinances, or rules of the board. (See Item 6 in Table 1.) Rules might well include a generalized recapitulation of such limitations and should logically extend to staff, as well as board members.

Language along lines indicated below should be adapted to fit accurately in local legislative framework, reminding board members and staff of limitations on their conduct.

Article 4. Conduct of Board Members, Staff

4.1 *Representation of Applicants or Appellants.*
No member of the board, or of its staff, shall represent applicants or appellants on matters on which the board is to make determinations.

This prohibition is so obvious it may appear unnecessary, but there have been instances of such actions. Including the prohibition in the rules settles the matter.

4.2. *Conflict of Interest.*
No member of the board shall participate in any case in which he has financial or personal interest in the property or action concerned, or will be directly affected by the decision, or has or believes he has any other conflict of interest as defined by applicable law. No member of the staff of the board or of any agency serving the board shall prepare or present arguments or reports, or attempt to influence decisions of the board, in any case in which he has similar interest.

Provisions concerning conflict of interest may be so completely covered in state law or local ordinance that mere cross-reference in rules will be adequate, but the above points should be covered somewhere.

4.2.1. *Chairman to Be Notified of Conflict of Interest; Actions by Chairman.*
As soon as any board member, or staff member of any agency serving the board, becomes aware of any potential conflict of interest in any case to come before the board, he shall notify the chairman or acting chairman of the particulars. Where the chairman finds that conflict clearly exists, he shall disqualify the board member from acting in the case and cause the secretary to enter the circumstances in the record and to make arrangements for such alternate services as are required.

Where the chairman or acting chairman has reasonable doubt as to whether the facts and applicable law indicate a degree of conflict justifying disqualification or excuse from service, he shall seek advice from counsel to the board. If counsel advises that, under the circumstances reported and applicable law, conflict appears to exist, the chairman shall proceed to disqualify or excuse as provided above. If counsel advises that there is reasonable doubt, the chairman may (a) disqualify or excuse the person involved, or (b) call for a determination by the board at a public meeting.

The record on any such determination by the board shall be full and complete and shall indicate the reasons supporting the board's decision.

It is probably not enough to say that a board or staff member *may* disqualify himself where there are conflicts. Disqualification should be mandatory, and as early as possible after potential conflict is perceived. The method should be spelled out, with procedures for determinations in borderline cases.

4.3. *Disqualification on Grounds of Influence Other Than at Public Hearing.*

A member may disqualify himself from voting whenever any applicant, or his agent, has sought to influence the vote of the member on his appeal or application, other than in the public hearing.[10]

This limitation may relieve the situation where applicants or attorneys have tended to exert influence privately prior to hearings. As a quasi-judicial body, the board should not be subject to such approaches.

4.4. *Expressions of Bias, Prejudice, or Individual Opinion Prior to Hearing and Determination.*

Board members may seek information from other members, the secretary, counsel to the board, or staff serving the board, prior to the public hearing, but no member shall discuss the case with any other parties thereto prior to the public hearing, or express any bias, prejudice, or individual opinion on proper judgment of the case prior to its hearing and determination. Violation of this rule shall be grounds for dismissal from the board.[11]

Board members should not express bias, prejudice, or individual opinion on cases prior to hearing and determination.

Where enabling legislation and/or court decisions establish such limitation (and under certain other circumstances), a further rule might be added:

4.5. *Members Not to Vote Unless Present at Hearing.*

No board member shall vote on any matter deciding an application or appeal except after attending the public hearing on the application or appeal.[12]

This language, legally sound in all states, may require modification in some where there are no provisions for alternates on the board and where more than a simple majority is required to reverse the decision of an administrative official or grant a variance or special exception. In cases where membership is set at five, for example, and a vote of four is necessary to reverse an administrative order or grant a variance or exception, absence of one member substantially changes the odds against applicants or appellants.

In these circumstances, if courts in the particular state have upheld later voting by absentees (as some have), the modification involved might run along these lines: "or has examined the full record of the hearing and based his determination thereon." In such instances, the member should support his individual vote with indications that he has indeed studied the record carefully.

Appeals and Applications

Powers and duties of the board are covered generally in the enabling act and more specifically in the zoning ordinance. It remains for the *Rules* to provide details on appeals and applications:

Article 5. Appeals and Applications; Filing; Time Limits; Information Required; Effects of Failure to Provide Required Information; Order at Hearings; Public Notice; Decisions

5.1. *Powers of the Board; Limitations; Procedures, Generally.*

The board shall have all and only such powers as are delegated to it by state enabling legislation and by the zoning ordinance and shall exercise such powers only in the manner, for the purposes, and in accordance with the procedures set forth therein.

5.2. *Filing Appeals and Applications; Forms; Time Limit on Appeals from Decisions of Administrative Officials.*

All appeals and applications shall be filed with the secretary on forms approved by the board. In addition to information required to identify persons and property involved, date and time of filing, and the like, such forms shall indicate the findings and determinations for which information is required, and the nature of information required to make such findings. On appeal from decisions of an administrative official, unless such official is also secretary of the board, notice of appeal shall also be filed with such official.

After introductory language, reminding the board that its powers are limited, the next subsection provides for double filing (as required by the Standard Act) on appeals alleging errors in decisions of the administrative officer, and sets time limits on such appeals. The next covers applications for special exceptions and appeals for variances. Following this, there is a catch-all subsection to cover situations where information submitted is incomplete:

5.2.1. *Appeals from Decisions of Administrative Officials.*

In the case of appeals from decisions of administrative officials, appeal must be taken within 30 days from the date of the written decision of such official and shall specify the alleged error or errors in such order, requirement, decision, or determination.

5.3. *Preliminary Determinations on Appeals and Applications Submitted for Filing; Deficiences in Information Supplied.*

When appeals and applications are submitted for filing, they shall be examined for completeness and accuracy, and particularly to determine whether all information necessary to make determinations has been supplied. Where information is lacking or inadequate at time of submission and the deficiency cannot be remedied immediately, the applicant or appellant shall be notified in writing as to the nature and extent of such deficiency, and the record shall be retained as an intent to appeal or apply until such deficiency is remedied. No docket number shall be assigned in such cases until required information has been supplied.

The language of 5.3 emphasizes the need for prompt and careful preliminary examination of documents for completeness and for establishing a written record on alleged deficiences (which might be important if *this* decision of an administrative officer is challenged). It also avoids cluttering the docket book with numbers unrelated to actual order for public hearing.

5.4. *Order of Appeals and Applications for Public Hearings.*

The secretary shall assign docket numbers to appeals and applications according to the date and time they were completed, and such numbers shall establish the order in which such cases shall be heard, provided that a case may be heard in advance of its order by concurrence of the same number of members of the board as is required to make a favorable determination on an appeal or application. Order may be deferred by request to the secretary at least five days prior to publication of public notice. After such date, order may be deferred only as provided at Section 12.3 of these *Rules,* "Deferrals and Continuances."

Continued cases shall be given priority over new cases except where the chair finds that circumstances of the continued case require a different order of hearing, in which event he shall assign such order in such a manner as to conclude the continued case as soon as is reasonably possible.

Standard Act provisions require the board to fix a "reasonable" time for the hearing, give public notice thereof, as well as notice to parties in interest, and make its decisions within a "reasonable time." The first "reasonable time" depends in part upon the public notice (how much in advance of the hearing?) and in part on time required to prepare cases. The second depends on anticipated procedures and time between regular meeting dates (with allowance for special meetings to cover contingencies). As a point of departure for local adaptation:

5.5.   *Time Limits on Public Hearings, Notice, Decisions.*

Appeals and applications shall be heard at public meetings within 45 days of date of assignment of docket numbers and decided at the same meeting, at the next regular meeting of the board, or at a special public meeting prior to such regular meeting, but in any event within 36 days of the meeting at which the hearing on the particular case was concluded.

Timing and manner of publication of public notice for such hearings shall be as provided in the zoning ordinance, at _____. In addition, at least 10 days in advance of the hearing, notice shall be given to parties in interest and to other persons required by the ordinance to be specially notified.

The flat 45-day limit avoids language like this: "Cases filed by 4 p.m. on the fourth Monday of the month shall be heard at the regular meeting of the next month (the fourth Wednesday after the first Monday)." The 36-day limit allows for variations in time resulting from such dating. Dating from time of docketing relates to §3.3.2.1 of rules cited on page 72.

The "other persons" notice requirement covers situations where the ordinance requires special notification of persons within a given distance of property involved.

Cross-referencing to zoning ordinance provisions on time and manner of publication of notice (including posting) will usually be adequate here. Otherwise, insert specific provisions.

Meetings and Public Hearings, Generally

Standard Act provisions indicate that meetings shall be held at the call of the chairman and at such other times as the board may determine. Where the work load of the board is light, this is a good arrangement. But in many jurisdictions, rules establish regular meeting dates, times, and places, with arrangements for cancellation. This encourages board members to reserve the regular date and tends to ensure a quorum. Rules may also provide for special meetings.

Here again, "model" provisions applicable to all states are almost impossible to contrive, and those below will need modification to fit local circumstances.

Article 6. Meetings, Hearings, Generally

6.1. *Regular Meetings.*

Regular meetings of the board shall be held at ____ p.m. at *(place)* on the *(day of the month, as first Tuesday, for example)*; provided that such meetings may be held at any other convenient place if directed by the chairman in advance of the meeting or upon a finding that such other location would serve public convenience or necessity.

6.2. *Special Meetings.*

Special meetings for any purpose may be held at the call of the chairman, or of (_____) members of the board. At least (_____) hours written notice of the time and place of any special meeting shall be given by the secretary except where written waivers of notice are filed by all members required to provide a quorum and in attendance at such meeting.

Call of a special meeting at a specified time and place and for specified purposes at a regular meeting shall be notice thereof as to members in attendance at such regular meeting, but other members shall receive written notice thereof.

If a special meeting is called on a case or cases subject to notice of hearing, the required notice provisions for the hearing shall be met.

6.3. *Recess or Adjournment.*

Any regular or special meeting may be recessed or adjourned from day to day, or to the time of any previously announced regular or special meeting, and such recess or adjournment to a time and place certain shall not require additional public notice.

6.4. *Cancellation.*

If no business is scheduled before the board, or if it is apparent that a quorum will not be available, any meeting may be cancelled by the chairman by giving notice to all members at least (____) hours before the time set for such meeting.[13]

6.5. *Quorum.*

A quorum of the board shall consist of (____) members, but the board shall not pass on any question relating to an appeal from a decision of any administrative official or upon any variance or special exception unless there are at least (____) members present.

The numbers supplied here will depend on enabling act language and particularly on the vote required to reverse an official or decide in favor of applicants or appellants. With a requirement for a five-member board and a four-fifth vote, three could handle routine board business (filling in the first blank), and four would be the minimum figure for the second. But four stacks the deck against applicants or appellants—they must convince 100 percent of the board members present. Where alternates may be used, it would be preferable to set the second figure at five.

All Meetings to Be Public

The Standard Act is clear and succinct in stating: "*All* meetings of the board shall **be** open to the public." (Emphasis supplied.) Formal public notice and hearing are required in connection with actions determining outcome of applications and appeals. Sunshine laws reenforce the mandate for public conduct of public business. Strict conformity with these rules reduces probability of successful legal challenge on procedural grounds. But . . .

What constitutes a "meeting"? If two board members have lunch together, have they transgressed? If the device of preliminary conference with applicants is used, what are the implications? When the board or a committee of the board views premises, may the public come along for the ride?

About Executive Sessions

No board ever got into *procedural* trouble by admitting the public to all of its official considerations and determinations on cases before it. "All meetings of the board shall be open to the public" would seem to indicate that there should be no meetings from which the public is barred. But practice departs from principle, and some courts and commentators find justification to support the departure—within strict limits.

If executive sessions (meetings of all or part of the members without the public present) are to be held, legality depends on what is done or considered during the session, timing in relation to public hearings, and what happens in public following the session.

Assuming that applicable sunshine laws do not prohibit executive sessions, case law and legal commentary establish guidelines to be used cautiously. Legal commentary often generalizes from cases in a few states, sometimes overlooking exceptions in others. This provides an uncertain foundation for opinion as to what the outcome might be in states where the matter has not been tested. With these caveats, some general principles are as follows:

1. **Don't hold an executive session prior to a hearing to discuss the merits of appeals or applications to come before the board.**   An Ohio

case (*Hardy v. Horst*, Ohio Com. Pl. 101 N.E.2d 398) serves as a point of departure for two comments.

Yorkely observes:

> Where a zoning ordinance provides that all of the meetings of the board . . . shall be open to the public, the board may not hold private meetings in advance of the regular meeting, regardless of the freedom of discussion the members might feel would be possible under such a plan. Such action is highly improper.[14]

Corpus Juris Secundum, a national legal reference encyclopedia, comes to the same conclusion, but is somewhat more specific as to the circumstances:

> A nonpublic meeting at the home of the chairman of the board held for the purpose of completely discussing, prior to the hearing, what the law is and any other factors which might come up is improper.[15]

2. Holding a (recessed) executive session during a public hearing, or an executive session after a public hearing, is permissible, so long as no new evidence is received and no official action is taken. According to Anderson:

> The requirement that a public hearing be held does not preclude the board of adjustment from meeting in executive session. The board may deliberate in private, but evidence must be received and official action must be taken and announced in public sessions.
>
> The requirement that a board of adjustment act only after public hearing assumes that it will act on the basis of the evidence adduced at such hearing. Thus, the evidence relied upon by the board must be introduced in the public hearing. The board may not rely upon information gained through interviews with public officials and examination of records outside the hearing room. Nor may the board rely upon reports received after the close of a public hearing. Reliance on evidence not adduced at the hearing amounts to a denial of a hearing and renders the action of the board subject to annulment by a court.

Anderson goes on to indicate that these rules are modified in practice to permit personal knowledge of board members to apply, and to allow for visits to premises and discussions with planning staff or the board's counsel, all outside the hearing room. In such cases, it would be well to report these grounds for decision at the hearing, and for the record.[16]

Corpus Juris Secundum sets some general rules:

> It has been held that a judicial or quasi-judicial proceeding of the board, or the deliberations of the board after a public hearing is completed, may take place in private.

Notes relating to this main entry set certain limitations:

Action taken by board of zoning appeals while in executive session with public excluded is illegal and void, and invalidity of such action is not cured by an announcement subsequently made at a public hearing, of action already taken at executive session.

Closed executive sessions may be held for purpose of deliberating as to what decision should be and at such session it is not improper for board to permit board's attorney to be present and solicit his legal advice with respect to issues raised by appeal.

And finally, under the heading "recess and deliberating session":

Ultimate order of board of adjustment would not be invalidated on ground that a recess and a deliberating session had been held among members of the board with no other persons present, where many hearings conducted in the matter were open to the public, where there was ample opportunity for interested persons to present any and all evidence and arguments, and where the final action of the board was adopted at an open hearing with all parties present.[17]

One reason for varying shades of interpretation appears in the copious case citations in footnotes. Decisions differ from state to state. But careful reading indicates a common theme. The board may, if it must, deliberate in private. It must act in public, and with the grounds for its decision made public:

3. **Formal action of the board must be in public meeting.**   Recording of evidence must be public. Findings of fact must be public. Determinations must be public. All these things must be done at a public meeting, with formal notice.

To clarify these matters, board *Rules* might run as follows:

6.6.   *Public Meetings of the Board; Notice; Other Activities of the Board; Schedule.*

All meetings of the board involving hearing of evidence and/or decisions of the board on appeals and applications shall be public, with formal notice as required by law.

Meetings for the conduct of other business of the board, including (*activities of the committee for preliminary review and other*) trips for viewing premises, shall not require such formal public notice and hearing, but shall be scheduled at least (____) days in advance, with the schedule posted in the office of the board.

Here a line has been drawn between meetings for *hearing* of evidence and making formal decisions, and activities related to routine board actions (what might be termed "housekeeping chores") including *collection* of evidence. Where no committee for preliminary review is established (see "Variation II, Committee for Preliminary Review," page 73), the material in parentheses should be eliminated.

6.7.   *Agenda, Order of Business.*

The secretary shall prepare an agenda for each board meeting. Order of business shall be as follows:

a. Call to order and roll call, with recording of members present and absent and indications as to whether absences are with consent of the chairman.

b. Continued hearings, with consideration and determination on cases as heard.

c. New hearings, with consideration and determination on cases as heard.

d. Action on minutes of previous meeting.

e. Old business.

f. New business.

g. Adjournment.

As to item *a*, indication as to whether absences are with consent of the chair relates to Section 2.3 of *Rules* discussed at page 66.

The order of business of this agenda is a departure from usual parliamentary form. Following roll call, action moves promptly to continued and then new hearings. This makes it unnecessary for the audience to sit through routine business.

There are several possible variations on timing of decisions. As proposed above, when the hearing on a case is concluded, the board proceeds immediately with its deliberations and makes its determination in public. Audience participation is out of order at this deliberative stage. The board has already heard. It must now decide. "Any person may appear" during the hearing, but not during decision making.

The North Carolina authors cited earlier have the following order of business, with decisions as the last item of business before adjournment: (a) roll call; (b) minutes; (c) hearing of cases; (d) reports of committees; (e) unfinished business; (f) new business; and finally (g) consideration and determination of cases heard. Their comment is that, under current interpretation of state law, the board could not exclude the public at this point, but that the chair should be firm in preventing audience comments or otherwise interfering with the board as it makes findings of facts and reaches its decision. "If individuals continue to interfere after being warned, they may be ordered to leave the meeting room and prosecuted for failure to do so. GS 143–318.7."[18] (It is apparent that these authors have had broad experience with audiences at board proceedings.)

In support of this approach, it is argued that it demonstrates a systematic pattern of procedure and reasoning applied to all of the cases involved. From the point of view of those members of the audience who want to hear how things turn out, it means a long wait through unrelated actions of limited interest to them.

For reasons outlined at pages 82–84, even where the executive session (recessed during a meeting or held afterwards) is permissible, the atmosphere for calm, judicial deliberation which may be argued as cause by board members may be seen by the public as an opportunity for hanky-panky. Decisions and supporting arguments must be in public in any case, at the same meeting with the hearing or at a meeting in the relatively near future (to conform to the 36-day limitation suggested at 5.5 [page 80]). Of the variations possible, this procedure is the least desirable. *Rules* 8.1, *Timing of Decisions*, suggests a flexible approach.

6.8.   *Application of* Robert's Rules of Order.

Except as otherwise specified by these *Rules*, parliamentary procedures of the board during meetings shall be in accord with *Robert's Rules of Order*.

Procedures at Hearings

Variations in rules concerning procedures at hearings reflect many influences. There are differences in legislative and judicial climate. There are differences in interpretation of enabling act language. (Thus, given "applicants *may* appear" at the hearing has been interpreted in some cases as "must," if they want to win. In others, and properly in our opinion, if the applicant or his agent does not appear, the case proceeds on the record indicated in the application and as established by other evidence presented.) There are differences according to the amount of pressure on the board. Heavy case loads tend to result in rules emphasizing brevity of presentation. Full airing of central and peripheral views may be fine if there are only one or two cases, but becomes a nightmare if there are 15.

In what follows, three principal sources are points of departure from which adaptations to the format used here and editorial revisions provide a smorgasboard for further selection and revision in local rules. "A Guide for Municipal Zoning Administration, with Forms," an Illinois publication, joins the Tucson and North Carolina sources.[19]

Article 7. Procedures at Hearings
The following rules shall apply in relation to hearings:

7.1. *Any Person May Appear or Be Represented; Authorization of Representatives.*

At the hearing, any person may appear or be represented by authorized agents or attorneys. Such agents or attorneys shall present competent evidence of extent of their authorization.

Standard Act language has been embellished in the first sentence by addition of the word "authorized." The second sentence is a further addition which experience indicates as desirable. At hearings, it is not unknown for individuals to attempt to enlarge the impact of their testimony by claiming to speak for groups which have taken no formal position on the matter involved, or are divided as to opinion. The board will want to know whether it hears one person's opinion or the concerted position of an organization.

7.2. *Witnesses to Testify Under Oath.*

All witnesses to material facts shall testify under oath, to be administered by the chair.

The North Carolina and Illinois sources (and many others) *require* the swearing of *all* witnesses. Tucson's chairman (like all others) is *empowered* to swear witnesses, but is not charged with doing so in all cases. If witnesses are to be sworn, arguments against swearing selectively appear in discussion at page 68.

The problem arises with statements from the floor. One person in the audience makes a statement including material facts not otherwise in evidence having bearing in the case. Another says, "We just don't think that would be appropriate in our neighborhood, with or without a hedge."

If the *Rule* reads as indicated, "All witnesses *to material facts* shall testify under oath," the cause of equity and the purposes of the board are served. The "official" witnesses are sworn as a matter of course. At the point where new material facts are introduced from the floor, the person proposing to introduce them is sworn, giving his testimony equal treatment. "With or without a hedge" opinions are accepted without being sworn to.

At this point, approaches begin to differ. Order for presenting evidence, as it appears in the Illinois *Guide*,[20] is used below in edited form and set in the numbering series for these *Rules*. Two items omitted are discussed following this entry. *Guide* material is the most complete and detailed of the three major sources, and alternate procedures will be discussed against this background:

7.3. *Order for Presenting Evidence.*

a. The applicant, appellant, or authorized representative may outline the nature of the request prior to introducing evidence. The chair may restate the case if this initial statement needs clarification.

b. Applicant presents evidence.

c. Objectors cross-examine.

d. Board members examine witnesses for applicant's side.

e. Objectors present evidence.

f. Applicants cross-examine.

g. Board members examine witnesses for objectors' side.

h. Rebuttal by applicant.

i. Rebuttal by objectors.

j. Evidence by board or its witnesses, including staff reports.[21]

Two items appearing in the Illinois *Guide* listing have been eliminated here. One is a provision that, if objectors retain counsel, such counsel must notify applicant's attorney and the board prior to the hearing. Absent such notice, *the applicant* may postpone the hearing to the next regular meeting of the board. Notification of representation may be a form of legal courtesy, but does not appear essential to a fair and impartial hearing. "This hearing is postponed because we didn't know the opposition had employed attorneys," says counsel for the applicant. Reaction of assembled objectors is predictable and justifiable. The chair might have some comments on jurisdiction.

The other item omitted permits submission of signed petitions favoring or opposing the proposed action, if prefaced only by a brief statement of position. The chair is in a position to decide whether such a petition is evidence material to findings required in the case. It is difficult to believe that it could be. If, as is generally agreed, a showing of hands pro and con at the hearing should not influence the decision (and is certainly bad practice), a petition having the same effect seems similarly immaterial.

As to order of presentation, Illinois puts evidence by the board and its witnesses, including staff reports, at the end. Tucson starts hearings on cases with the zoning administrator's report.[22] The North Carolina authors have an initial preliminary statement of the case by "the chairman, or such person as he may direct."[23]

Common practice begins the hearing with presentation of evidence available to the board, including staff reports. This may help in reducing repetitious evidence later by presenting information on which both sides may agree (or from which there may be specific disagreement on details). Duplication of effort and repetitious testimony might be further reduced if staff reports are available in advance of the hearing, as suggested in note 21 appearing on page 105.

Variation I adjusts to these changes and has the applicant outlining the nature of his case as he begins presenting his evidence:

Variation I

7.3.   *Order for Presenting Evidence.*

a. The chair, or such persons as he may direct, describes the nature of the case, and evidence available to the board is presented, including staff reports.

b. The applicant or appellant outlines the nature of the request and presents supporting evidence.

(Item *j* is eliminated. Items *c* through *i* remain unchanged.)

Concerning cross-examination of witnesses, Attorney Marlin Smith argues in "Play Fair in Public Hearings"[24] that if a hearing is regarded by state law as quasi-judicial, all parties must have the opportunities to cross-examine opponents' witnesses, and notes an Illinois decision requiring an opportunity for cross-examination in a rezoning hearing. (Rezoning would normally be outside the scope of a board's activities, but some strange things have happened in Illinois.) The Illinois *Guide* rules make provision specifically for cross-examination.

The North Carolina authors apparently consider the matter settled there: "All witnesses before the board shall be placed under oath and the opposing party may cross-examine them."[25]

In a major case, with counsel serving the board and attorneys representing applicants and opposing groups, orderly and enlightening cross-examination of witnesses is a possibility—just. Those familiar with ordinary hearings before boards may view with alarm cross-examination of applicant's and opposing witnesses by the other side, particularly if lawyers are in short supply.

Tucson's board was established by Ordinance No. 4299, which states that it is a quasi-judicial body. Its *Rules* have apparently been tempered in the fires of debate. The section on hearings contains these paragraphs:[26]

Order of debate: Orderly procedure requires that each side shall proceed without interruption by the other; that all arguments and pleadings shall be addressed to the board; and that there be no questioning or argument between individuals.

Board and staff's remarks: During the hearing, the chairman, board members, and members of the staff may ask questions and make appropriate comments pertinent to the case; however, no member should debate or argue an issue with the applicant.

Applicant (and others) questioned: The chairman and board members may direct any questions to the applicant or any person speaking in order to bring out all relevant facts, and may call for questions from members of the staff.

Here there is to be no cross-examination of applicant's witnesses by objectors or vice versa and "no questioning or argument between individuals" (presumably those in the audience—the board could hardly be so constrained). The board will conduct any examination of witnesses it deems necessary after hearing their presentations.

Where rules are drawn in states in which cross-examination has not been set as a requirement by state law or court decision (a matter on which competent legal advice should be sought before proceeding far), Variation II is a possibility, eliminating the reference to cross-examination.

Variation II

As for either language first indicated or Variation I, but with items concerning cross-examination eliminated.

About evidence, material and irrelevant. *Rules* generally include language along the following lines concerning evidence, and that is probably all they need to include:

7.4. *Evidence.*

The board shall not be bound by strict rules of evidence, not limited to consideration of such evidence as would be admissible in a court of law, but it may exclude irrelevant, immaterial, incompetent, or unduly repetitious testimony or evidence. The chair shall rule on all questions relating to the admissibility of evidence, but may be overruled by a majority of the board members present.

Wording here is a composite of provisions from the Illinois *Guide*[27] and the North Carolina text.[28] If the chair is in doubt as to admissibility, these notes might be helpful:

Screening evidence at hearings. Evidence at hearings is for the purpose of determining whether required findings can be made. Required findings are all the findings that need be made. Evidence which does not relate to required findings is irrelevant and immaterial. When there is sufficient valid evidence to support a required finding, more is superfluous.

Conduct during the hearing; interrogations. Tucson provisions cited above would be a useful addition to any *Rules* and are adapted for these:

7.5. *Conduct During Hearings; Interrogations.*

During the hearing, each side shall proceed without interruption by the other. All arguments and pleadings shall be addressed to the chair. There shall be no questioning or argument between individuals in the audience.

The chair or board members, counsel to the board, or staff may direct any questions to the applicant, witnesses, or any person speaking from the audience, to bring out pertinent facts. The chair or board members may call for pertinent facts from the staff, or make appropriate comments pertinent to the case. No board member should debate or argue with persons in the audience.

Findings and Decisions

State law, the zoning ordinance, and board *Rules* have set general requirements concerning findings and determinations of the board—time limits for action, findings required, and the like. At this point, *Rules* need only to detail actions on decisions in individual cases.

Taking into account the considerations raised below on timing of decisions, the first provisions indicate preferential priorities, but allow flexibility in adjusting to circumstances. It should be emphasized that there are two phases involved here, first the hearing and *after its conclusion* the determination. Full audience participation is wanted at the hearing, but the board should be uninterrupted by the audience during deliberations. The chair should make this distinction clear early, and as often as necessary.

Timing of decisions *should* depend on two variables—complexity of cases (simple to involved) and length of the agenda (short to long). The attitude of the audience may also be a factor—if unruly or contentious, the chair may decide to let attrition bring relief as hearings on individual cases drag on and routine business of the board proceeds, leaving determinations on cases to the end, or delaying until the next regular or special meeting.

Article 8. Findings and Decisions, Individual Cases or Classes of Cases

After conclusion of the hearing on the case, within the time limits set by Section 5.5 of these *Rules*, the board shall examine the evidence before it in relation to findings required and make its decision. More particularly:

8.1.   *Timing of Decisions.*

With due consideration to the length of the agenda, the nature of the case, the complexity of the evidence, and the findings required, the chair may elect, subject to being overruled by a majority of the board in attendance on motion duly passed:

a. To proceed immediately to determination and decision on conclusion of the hearing in the particular case, or

b. To defer determination and decision until later in the same meeting, or

c. To defer determination and decision until a specified special or regular meeting of the board within the time limit set by these *Rules.*

In the course of determinations under *a* or *b*, above, should it be found advantageous to defer further determination or decision in the case for good cause stated, the chair may elect or the board may move to continue such determinations and decisions to a later time in the same meeting or to a specified special or regular meeting.

That sets guidelines but leaves room to maneuver. The only sure thing about public hearings is unpredictability. The chair assumes that a decision will be fairly simple and wants to get it out of the way. Complications set in and a large audience is waiting to get on to other things. He decides, or the board moves, to continue the particular session to a general deliberative action at the end of the agenda. The hearings grind on, and the board wears down. Toward midnight, the chair elects or the board moves to continue to a special meeting, or the next regular meeting.

8.2.   *Findings and Decisions, by Classes of Cases.*

8.2.1.   *Appeals from Decisions of Administrative Officer.*

If at least (____) members of the board concur in a finding of error in any decision, order, requirement, or determination of the administrative officer appealed from, the decision shall be favorable to the appellant. Such decision by the board shall specify the decision, order, requirement, or determination which should have been made, and the decision of the board shall be binding upon the administrative officer.

8.2.2.   *Special Exceptions.*

If at least (____) members of the board concur that the evidence supports favorable findings on the application for a special exception before it, or that such findings could be made if conditions and safeguards were established, the decision shall be favorable to the applicant, provided that such conditions and safeguards as may be required for such favorable finding, as specified in the decision, shall be binding upon the applicant and his successors in interest.

8.2.3.   *Variances.*

If at least (____) members of the board concur that the evidence supports favorable findings on the appeal for a variance before it, or that such findings could be made if conditions and safeguards were established, the decision shall be favorable to the applicant, provided that such conditions and safeguards as may be required for such favorable finding, as specified in the decision, shall be binding upon the appellant and his successors in interest.

Numbers to be inserted in the blanks will be set by state law. The Standard Act requires four.

8.3.   *Form and Procedure for Decisions.*

All such decisions of the board shall be made at a public meeting by motion made and seconded and by roll call vote. The motion shall be in the form of findings of fact and shall state the reasons for the findings by the board. If the grant of a special exception or variance includes conditions or safeguards, such conditions and safeguards, and the reasons therefor, shall be stated in the motion.[29]

Rule 8.3, adapted from the Illinois *Guide*, is a clear and complete statement of procedures and content required in a motion on decision. As described, the motion includes all of the elements usually involved in appeals to the courts from board decisions.

Framing such a motion sounds like a formidable job, particularly in complicated cases. It would be, if approached on a case-by-case basis. This is why forms are important. Properly designed, they organize findings required and supporting evidence to facilitate making findings and decisions.

Notification of Decisions

Article 9. Notification of Decisions.

Notice of the board decision shall be given to the applicant or appellant and to the administrative officer, and to other interested parties who have requested such notice, by the secretary of the board as soon as reasonably possible after the decision is reached, but within (____) days.

Records

The North Carolina text is adapted here for wording on records of cases:[30]

Article 10.   Records of Cases

10.1   *Content of Records of Individual Cases.*

The decision of the board shall be shown in the record of the case. Such record shall show the reasons for the determination, with a summary of the evidence introduced and the findings of fact made by the board.

10.1.1 *Cases Involving Appeals from Decision of Administrative Officer.*

Records of cases in which appeals resulted in decisions either to affirm or to reverse decisions of the administrative officer shall indicate supporting reasoning and in the case of reversal shall specify the decision, order, requirement, or determination to apply.

10.1.2. *Special Exceptions.*

Where a special exception is granted, the record shall state ir detail facts supporting required findings and shall also detail conditions and safeguards imposed by the board, if any, with reasons for such imposition. Where a special exception is denied, reasons for such denial shall be indicated in detail.

10.1.3. *Variances.*

Where a variance is granted, the record shall state in detail the nature of the hardship found to exist by the board, and shall also detail conditions and safeguards imposed by the board, if any, with reasons for such imposition. Where a variance is denied, reasons for such denial shall be indicated in detail.

10.2 *Records to Be Entered in Minutes of the Board; Advance Distribution of Draft of Minutes to Board Members; Approval; Authentication.*

Such record shall be entered in the minutes of the board. A draft of proposed minutes containing such records shall be transmitted to each board member at least (_____) days in advance of the meeting at which they are to be considered for approval. Following approval, as submitted or as amended, the minutes shall be acknowledged as to accuracy by the signature of the chairman and the secretary.

Comment in the North Carolina text states: "This is a very important rule. It is necessary for the decision to be very complete, giving a full account of the reasons on which it is based, in order to give the court a proper picture of the case in the event of an appeal from the board's decision. Otherwise it may be necessary for the court to call upon the board to make additional findings. The board's decision may be overturned solely because the court finds that the board has made insufficient findings to support its decision."[31]

Beyond that, it is probable that, where a board is otherwise performing properly, likelihood of attack in court diminishes as quality of records improves, and vice versa.

North Carolina provisions have been altered and amended in some details in the *Rules* above. The provisions concerning denials of special exceptions and variances have been added. Reasons for denial might be as important in court attacks as those for granting (depending on direction from which the attack comes).

The requirement that drafts of minutes *containing records of decisions* be provided members in advance of meetings in which they are to be approved is also added. This gives members time to read and note corrections, which would be difficult if they didn't receive their copies before the meeting started, and should substantially reduce time spent in processing minutes at meetings which also include hearings. Approval of minutes which are this important should not be taken lightly.

Expiration of Special Exceptions, Variances

Many *Rules* provide that unless action permitted (a building permit issued, a use begun, a certificate of occupancy issued) is initiated within (___) days, the special exception or variance authorizing the action expires. Two escape hatches may be used. Thus in Tucson, "The building inspector may grant a single 90-day extension for good cause."[32] Or the wording setting the general time limit may begin "Unless otherwise specified by the board. . . ."

The North Carolina text comments: "This rule is designed to prevent the board's being flooded with cases wherein property owners apply for a variance or an exception before shopping around for a purchaser for their property, hoping that the variance will give their property a more attractive status. The board has enough to do without taking on this function of assisting in the sale of property. A time limitation on the effective life of its action will tend to encourage property owners to wait until they are actually ready to build or to use the property for the purpose cited in the application before applying for a variance or an exception."[33]

The board is authorized to establish conditions and safeguards. Usually these are set in individual cases after examining the circumstances of the case, to alter foreseen conditions so that proposals become acceptable in light of findings which must be made.

Consider three conditions or safeguards: "Parking and loading areas must be located at the side of the building, away from the adjoining residential district, to protect residents from adverse views and noise." "A marginal access road must be constructed along the front of the property to minimize conficts with traffic on Liberty Avenue and reduce traffic hazards." "A building permit must be obtained within 60 days of the date of this action or the special exception expires because the applicant's motives may have been speculative."

One of those statements does not seem grounded in public purposes of zoning, or related to findings the board is required to make.

It would seem preferable to permit setting individual expiration dates, if appropriate, and to relate termination time to circumstances of the case. Assuming a major shopping center proposal eligible under special exception, there might quite possibly be speculative elements—for example, a contract for sale of the land conditioned on "getting the zoning." Does this alter the findings the board is required to make? Should a time limit be set *because of this consideration*? No, in both cases. But there are other valid reasons for setting a time limit. If one of the findings involves service of public convenience, failure to build after grant of the special exception may block service of public convenience elsewhere in the area. Time allowed before expiration should be established according to time needed to proceed diligently with preparation of building plans and apply for a permit, and should probably cover more than issuance of the permit.

"Unless otherwise specified by the board," as included in usual language, would allow for this relation between regulation and purpose, but the flat 60-, 90-, or 180-day expiration applying in other cases still lacks justification.

At the other extreme, a side-yard variance is granted on a narrow lot. The owner does not build within 60 days. The variance expires. The lot is sold. The new owner applies for a side-yard variance. This *reduces* the work load of the board? If unique circumstances create a hardship justifying a variance on a particular piece of property, and the unique circumstances and hardship are likely to continue indefinitely, why should not the variance continue indefinitely?

(It seems likely that the termination clause may have crept into common language in rules or ordinances because of use variances. The use variance has been increasingly prohibited by state laws or local ordinances, and should be. Narrowness of a lot does not justify a grocery in a residential neighborhood. But if a misguided or uninstructed board does issue a use variance, a time limitation set in the particular case might be appropriate.)

As another consideration, application for a building permit does not necessarily assure anything but application for a building permit. The devious speculator with large financial gains at stake applies for and receives a building permit and sits on it, without starting construction.

He has protected his rear by satisfying the letter of the requirement, but there has not been corresponding protection of public purposes and interest.

So the rules concerning expiration should require findings on a case-by-case basis, should relate time limits (if any) to valid public purposes, and should be framed to accomplish those purposes fully and fairly. It may well be that only part of the actions proposed will require time limits. Priority of actions may affect public interest more than time of actions.

Expiration may have serious consequences not only for the applicant or appellant but also for the public. The partially completed townhouses or the walls of the shopping center stand vacant, attractive nuisances for children, a temptation to vandals, a haunt for vagrants. Must they be removed unless completed? By whom, and at whose expense? Is a performance bond indicated, and for what should it be used on forfeiture? Under what circumstances should deadlines be extended, and by whom?

Article 11. Establishing Priorities of Action and Time Limits on Special Exceptions and Variances; Performance Bonds or Sureties; Expiration of Time Limits; Extensions

As conditions attached to a special exception or variance, and on findings supporting public necessity for such conditions, the board may:

11.1. *Priorities for Actions.*

Establish priorities for all or part of the actions proposed in relation to the special exception or variance, and/or

11.2. *Setting Time Limits.*

Set time limits within which all or part of the actions proposed shall be begun and/or completed.

11.3. *Performance Bonds or Other Sureties.*

As part of such conditions relating to time limits, require performance bonding or other surety in amount and form appropriate to the circumstances of the case (*or* as generally required in connection with subdivision in the jurisdiction). Such bonding or other surety may also be required to assure continued maintenance of facilites required as conditions or safeguards.

11.4. *Expiration of Time Limits; Effects.*

Upon expiration of time limits, unless extension is granted as provided below, the special exception or variance shall expire and become void, together with all permits issued pursuant thereto, and construction shall cease except where the administrative official determines that stay of further construction would cause imminent peril to life or property, in which case construction under the permit shall continue until such peril is removed.

Where time limits have expired, and special exceptions or variances have been voided, construction or use of the property shall be only as permitted generally within the district without special exception or variance (as applicable) unless a new special exception or variance is granted.

11.5. *Extension of Time Limits.*

In establishing time limits, the board shall indicate in each case whether, how, and how often such limits may be extended, circumstances to be considered in allowing such extension, and limitations on periods for extension, as appropriate. Unless otherwise indicated, applications for extension must be made at least (_____) days before time limits expire.

Article 11 *Rules*, above, may be considerably more than will be needed in most jurisdictions. They relate to relatively complex forms of development which *may* be handled as special exceptions—planned developments, mobile home parks, cluster developments, for example. If so handled, provisions like these may be already covered in the zoning ordinance and would not need repetition in board *Rules*, although they might be handled by reference.

As to details, establishing priorities of action may often be important even where there are no time limits. Thus in a planned development involving both housing and a shopping center, the board might require the housing element to proceed first. Otherwise the planned development device may be used to establish a shopping center where one would not otherwise be permitted.

As should now be clearly apparent, setting time limits can be tricky and troublesome. Merely requiring a building permit or a use permit doesn't solve the problem. As stated, the rule allows the board to pick and choose. If there are elements which are really vital, and setting an order of priorities won't take care of the situation, time limits can be applied to those elements only, leaving the developer with flexibility to respond to crises in marketing, housing demand, interest rates, and the like as he judges best. Developers have an ample supply of troubles of their own, without adding unnecessary regulatory deadlines to them.

On the matter of performance bonds or other sureties (flexibility in choice should be allowed here, too), these have long been required under subdivision regulations, and similar requirements are on the increase in relation to various forms of planned developments in which provision or maintenance of facilities, including common open space and perhaps private sewage treatment plants, is to be a common responsibility of the occupants or run by management privately. Where subdivision regulation requirements for sureties are working out well, the language in parentheses may simplify things for the board, and for developers.

On expiration of time limits, our three major sources are silent as to effects. This is probably on the assumption that, if a building permit has not been issued, there's no harm done. As demonstrated, concern should extend considerably beyond whether or not a building permit is issued. Remedies for public peril are mandated in Standard Act language lifted out of its original context under appeals from decisions of administrative officers. Remedies for applicants may or may not help them—they can do whatever they could have done in the district without the special exception or variance, or they can apply for a new special exception or variance. Rules for rehearings of cases denied, discussed later, will not limit the timing of such actions because their applications or appeals were not denied, but voided after grant.

As to extension of time limits, *Rule* 11.5 allows the board to temper its approach to the circumstances of individual cases, but terms should be set at the time of the original decision. Possible variations include extension permitted by the administrative official for specified reasons and for a set period, with further extension only by board action, or extension by the board after it has looked into the problem.

Requests to Withdraw or Amend Appeals or Applications

For reasons stated at page 26, tactical withdrawals after the hearing session is begun should be discouraged. To this end, wording similar to that quoted from the proposed Atlanta ordinance at page 28 is used in the *Rules* below. (As indicated previously, if entries in the ordinance are adequate, cross-referencing in the *Rules* is all that's needed.)

Amendment is another matter. It should be permitted at any time before the board makes its decision unless deferral or continuation of a hearing is involved. If an applicant appears at the scheduled hearing and requests deferral before presenting his case so that he may have time to prepare an amendment, or if in the course of hearing procedures he requests continuation of the case for the same reason, several issues arise.

The first is the nature of the amendment. If trivial, the board may deny the request. Thus if it appears that the applicant may be using the amendment ploy as a delaying tactic, the board might elect to proceed with the case. If the amendment the applicant wants to work out involves no "substantial" change and the board lets him go ahead, the case may be deferred or continued to a specified date. If the change is "substantial," new public notice is indicated, so no date need be specified when the request is granted.

"Substantial" is used here in the same special sense which applies in relation to zoning amendments. It is generally held after a proposed amendment has been advertised for zoning hearing and the hearing proceeds, the amendment passed must be the amendment given notice and heard. Thus in actions immediately preliminary to adoption the governing body may not shift the boundaries, enlarge the area involved, or increase the range of uses permitted. If it proposes such "substantial" change, there must be new notice and hearing.

On the other side of this coin, courts have been known to uphold such changes where the area is reduced or restrictions increased.

Proposed zoning amendments and proposed amendments to applications and appeals don't run exactly parallel, of course, because of the nature and detail of public notice. There is enough similarity, however, to suggest caution. When in doubt, the chair (or the board) should require new notice.

As a technical note, there is nothing sacred about five days as the breakpoint in these provisions or in *Rules* 5.4, but there should be *some* lead time. To say merely "before public notice is published" won't do. If the press run is on, it's too late to hold back the notice. If the notice is run, it's too late to hold back the public.)

Article 12.   Requests to Withdraw or Amend Appeals or Applications; to Defer or Continue Hearings

12.1.   *Withdrawal.*

On written request from the appellant, applicant, or authorized agent, an appeal or application may be withdrawn at any time before the board makes its decision in the case. If such request is made less than five days before scheduled publication of public notice, limitations on resubmittal of substantially the same appeal or application shall be the same as in cases where appeals or applications are denied.

12.2.   *Amendment.*

12.2.1.   *Requests Delivered to Secretary Five Days Prior to Scheduled Publication of Notice.*

Applicants, appellants, or their authorized agents may amend applications or appeals in any lawful manner on written request delivered to the secretary of the board not less than five days prior to scheduled publication of public notice. Where such requests are received, the secretary shall so indicate in the docket book, and shall not cause notice of the hearing to be published, nor place the case on the hearing agenda, until the amendment has been received.

12.2.2. Other Requests.

Other requests to amend applications or appeals shall be made in writing to the secretary prior to the hearing, or to the board at the hearing, and shall include the amendment if prepared, or the nature and purpose of an amendment to be prepared and time required for preparation.

If the request to amend is denied, with cause for such denial stated in the motion, hearing and decision on the case shall proceed.

If the amendment has been prepared and the request to amend is granted, the board shall make a finding as to whether there is substantial difference between the case as it has been described in public notice and the case as amended. If substantial difference is found, new public notice shall be required, with fees paid by the applicant, before the hearing of the case may proceed.

The board shall also determine whether the nature of the amendment is such as to require referral for reexamination by counsel or staff members having made reports on the original application or appeal. If such referral is found necessary, the board may proceed with the hearing or may continue it to a time and place specified, but shall not decide the case until it has considered the response.

If the amendment has not been prepared and the request to amend is granted, the board shall make similar findings and requirements if the amendment as described generally appears likely to create substantial difference. Upon receipt of the amendment, the board may make referrals for reexamination deemed necessary. If new public notice is required, the board shall defer any further hearing on the case until the requirement has been met. If no new public notice is required, the board may take such action as seems appropriate on deferring or continuing the hearing, but shall specify a date and place, with due regard to reasonable time requirements of the appellant or applicant.

12.3. Deferrals and Continuances.

On its own motion, or on approval of requests by applicants, appellants, or their authorized agents, the board may defer the hearing of cases or provide for later continuance of cases on which hearings have begun. Such deferrals or continuances shall be permitted only for good cause, stated in the motion, and, unless time and place is stated, shall require new public notice, with fees paid by applicants or appellants if deferrals or continuances are at their request or result from their actions.

If many people in the audience are interested in a case, it should not be deferred without really compelling reasons. If at all possible, proceed with the hearing, let them present their evidence and air their views, and then continue the hearing to another meeting.

Refilings; Rehearings

Once the board has decided a case, *substantially the same case* should not be allowed to come before it again. Ever. The proper appeal from a decision of the board is to the courts, not to a later board. But many rules or ordinances permit rehearing of substantially the same case after a specified period, usually one or two years. In the *Rules* which follow, there is no permission to rehear the same case.

But how much change must there be, and what kind, before a case becomes no longer substantially the same as its forerunner? And how should the judgment be made? The North Carolina text provides a method which focuses this determination and should save applicants a great deal of time and effort. Adapted for these *Rules*, it reads like this:

Article 13.   Rehearings

13.1.   *Applications for Rehearings.*

Applications for rehearings shall be filed with the secretary of the board. Evidence in support of the application shall initially be limited to that necessary to enable the board to determine whether there has been a substantial change in the facts, evidence, or conditions in the case.

13.2.   *Determination by the Board.*

Within 36 days of acceptance of the application by the secretary, the board shall make its determination on the application for rehearing. The application shall be denied by the board if it finds from the record that there has been no substantial change in the facts, evidence, or conditions in the case. If the board finds that there has been a change, the applicant shall be authorized to submit a new application or appeal.[34.]

A simple majority of the board is required for such findings.

13.3.   *Effect of Rehearings on Appeals to the Courts.*

The filing of an application for rehearing shall stop the running of the (____) day period in which petition to the court must be made. In such event, the period shall run from the date of denial of the application for rehearing, if denied, or from the (*date*) decision following the rehearing is filed in the office of the board.

The final paragraph here is picked from the Tucson *Rules.*[35] Standard Act language limits the period for petition to the court to 30 days from filing of the decision of the board. The provision above keeps the possibility of appeal alive for the applicant. Without it, any part of the 30-day period remaining to him when he makes his application for rehearing would be lost while the board considers the matter.

There seems no reason why a public hearing (with full-scale notice) should be required in connection with determinations as to whether rehearings should be permitted, and decision by simple majority is probably safe if authorized in *Rules*. If the ordinance sets procedural requirements on rehearing applications, Standard Act wording raises the requirement to four: "The concurring vote of four members of the board . . . shall be necessary . . . to decide in favor of the applicant on *any* matter on which it is required to pass *under any such ordinance*." (Emphasis supplied.)

Amendment of Rules; Waiving or Suspending Rules

Rules should not be amended on the spur of the moment or waived arbitrarily. They may neither be amended nor waived on matters set by state law or the zoning ordinance.

Article 14. Amending or Waiving Rules

14.1. *Amending Rules.*

These rules may be amended by a majority of the board except where such amendment would be contrary to requirement or limitations set by state law or the zoning ordinance. An amendment may be proposed at any regular meeting of the board, and shall not be acted upon until the following regular meeting. Not less than seven days prior to the meeting at which the amendment is to be voted upon, members shall be sent a copy of such proposed change.

14.2. *Waiving or Suspending Rules.*

A rule of procedure may be suspended or waived at any meeting by unanimous vote of board members present unless such rule is set by state legislation or the zoning ordinance.

Notes

1. Wisconsin Stats., Counties, §59.99 (3).

2. Code of Virginia, 1950, Title 15.1., Chapter 11, §15.1-494.

3. Alaska General Statutes, Title 29, §29.33.110.

4. Code of Virginia, 1950, Title 15.1., Chapter 11, §15.1-496.2, amended in 1983.

5. Georgia General Planning Act of 1957, as revised through 1969, Section 11.

6. California Government Codes, Title 7, Chapter 4, Article 3, §65900–65904.

7. Ordinance No. 4299, adopted Dec. 23, 1974, Section 23–505.1.B. Appears as Appendix A, City of Tucson, *Board of Adjustment Rules and Regulations and City Code Provisions Relating to Board of Adjustment*, adopted in 1964, as amended through 1975 (cited as Tucson *Rules*).

8. Except for the last sentence here, this and the two previous subsections are adapted from the Tucson *Rules*. These are well-constructed and unusually detailed, and amendments indicate where testing over a long period has suggested tightening or improvement. (The provision on appointment of alternates does not appear in the Tucson *Rules*.)

9. To this point, "Duties of the Secretary" is taken with minor modifications from Tucson *Rules*.

10. Tucson *Rules*, under "Decisions of the Board."

11. Michael B. Brough and Philip P. Green, Jr., *The Zoning Board of Adjustment in North Carolina* (Chapel Hill: Institute of Government, University of North Carolina, 1978), adapted from language at p. 46, "Rules of Conduct for Members" (cited as *Board of Adjustment in North Carolina*).

12. *Board of Adjustment in North Carolina*, p. 46.

13. *Board of Adjustment in North Carolina*, pp. 46–7.

14. E. C. Yokeley, *Zoning Law and Practice* (Charlottesville, Va.: The Michie Co., 3rd ed., 1965, with supplements), Vol. 2, §13–9, p. 92.

15. Robert M. Anderson, *American Law of Zoning* (Rochester, N.Y.; Cooperative Publishing Co., 1st ed., 1976), Vol. 3, p. 213.

16. Corpus Juris Secundum 101A, *Zoning and Land Planning*, (St. Paul, Minn.: West Publishing Co., 1979) §188, p. 556 (cited as CJS).

17. CJS, §188, p. 556, citing *Harvey v. Horst*, as noted; *Orange Co. Publications Division of Ottoway Newspapers, Inc. v. Council of City of Newburgh*, 393 N.Y.S.2d 298, affirmed 411 N.Y.S.2d 564; *Dupont Circle Citizens Ass'n v. D.C. Bd. of Zoning Adjustment*, 364 A.2d 610; *Sullivan v. Northwest Garage and Storage Co.*, 165 A.2d 881, 223 Md. 544; and *Mueller v. City of Phoenix ex rel Phoenix Bd. of Adjustment II*, 435 P.2d 472, 102 Ariz. 575.

18. *Board of Adjustment in North Carolina*, pp. 47–8.

19. R. Marlin Smith, Clyde W. Forrest, Jr., and Eric C. Freund, *A Guide for Municipal Zoning Administration, with Forms* (Urbana–Champaign: Department of Urban and Regional Planning, University of Illinois, 1972), pp. 82–3, (cited as Illinois *Guide*).

20. Illinois *Guide*, pp. 82–3.

21. Marlin Smith, one of the Illinois *Guide* authors, notes that "a common breach of disclosure requirement is the practice of considering, at the hearing,

staff reports that have not been made available to the public in advance," in "Play Fair in Public Hearings," a *Commissioner's Memo* in *Planning* (Chicago: American Planning Association), Vol. 49, No. 3, March 1983, pp. 10–11, (cited as "Play Fair"). Such reports might well be required to be available in the board office a few days before the hearing. The entire *Commissioner's Memo* appears as Appendix **A**.

22. Tucson *Rules*, p. 9.

23. *Board of Adjustment in North Carolina*, p. 49.

24. "Play Fair," p. 9.

25. *Board of Adjustment in North Carolina*, p. 49.

26. Tucson *Rules*, p. 10.

27. Illinois *Guide*, p. 83.

28. *Board of Adjustment in North Carolina*, p. 49.

29. Illinois *Guide*, p. 83.

30. *Board of Adjustment in North Carolina*, p. 50.

31. *Board of Adjustment in North Carolina*, p. 50.

32. Tucson *Rules*, p. 14.

33. *Board of Adjustment in North Carolina*, p. 50.

34. Tucson *Rules*, p. 49.

35. Tucson *Rules*, p. 16.

5

Improved Current Zoning Practice

Things have changed considerably since the Standard Act began its influence on zoning. The best of current zoning practice reflects the change.

Governments now perform more functions and employ more specialists. Planning commissions are now common, and many jurisdictions now have professional planning staffs and/or consultant assistance.

Zoning "in accordance with a comprehensive plan" no longer means merely that the entire area of the jurisdiction should be zoned.[1] The law of zoning is more sharply defined—and on many more points—although contradictory opinions sometimes blur the focus. With experience, there have been improvements in zoning techniques and in the way zoning is administered.

Continuing Need for Performance of Board Functions

Even with substantial improvements, zoning seems unlikely to reach that peak of perfection where every contingency is foreseen, every provision is open to only one interpretation, and no property is of such a character that regulations work undue and unnecessary hardship to its owner. The functions which have been performed by the board must still be performed, and, to a considerable extent, the board will continue to perform them. The move toward trained professional zoning examiners as supplements to, or substitutes for, boards of adjustment, has much to recommend it, but isn't making as much headway as might be desired.

Much can be done to lighten the board's work load, to simplify matters for applicants for permits, to expedite processing, and to improve the chances for equitable treatment of those appearing before the board.

State Enabling Legislation and Local Zoning

Some improvements require changes from Standard Act language; some can be made at either the state level (to apply generally) or in individual local ordinances; and some must be handled locally.

To illustrate the relationships between state enabling legislation and local regulations, assume a situation in which state enabling legislation is silent on conflict of interest and qualifications of board members. Membership of the board is limited to five members, with three-year terms and no provision for overlaps. A four-fifths vote is required to decide in favor of an applicant or appellant.

A local jurisdiction may include limitations applying to conflicts of interest, and establish qualifications for board members without amendment of Standard Act language. (A word of caution is in order here. Many state zoning enabling acts will not require specific provisions on conflicts of interest in zoning cases because of generally applicable state statutes affecting a broad spectrum of boards and public officials. In such instances, special treatment in zoning enabling legislation may be superfluous, but the local ordinance or rules of the board may well make note of the general statute.) But it may not alter the other elements in the combination cited above unless enabling language is changed accordingly.

It may be very desirable to provide for alternate members and to indicate the manner in which they are to serve in the absence of regular members or their inability to vote because of conflict of interest or for other reasons. This cannot be done locally unless state enabling legislation authorizes it (which some does). Another expedient is to reduce division required to favor an applicant to a simple majority. Here again, state sanction is required (and some states have provided it, although this is a less desirable move than the one indicated above, which usually retains the necessity for more than simple majority).

Certainly no change in Standard Act language is necessary before inserting local requirements as to findings to be made in connection with variances or general or specific standards to be met on special exceptions. On variances, the better local ordinances (and a number of state enabling acts) have tightened and expanded upon brief and uncertain original Standard Act wording. But if the jurisdiction is governed by language unchanged from that in the Standard Act, the local legislative body would overstep its authority if it took upon itself or assigned to any other agency than the board of adjustment the function of granting variances. (Here again, a few states have made changes authorizing the legislative body of the planning commission to perform part of original board functions. Most informed observers consider involvement of the legislative body in administrative or appellate matters to be undesirable.)[2]

Obviously, some actions must be handled entirely locally rather than directly controlled by state enabling legislation. These include decisions as to which uses shall be permitted within particular districts by right, made permissible by special exception, or handled by routine or special procedures by administrative personnel.

With these ground rules established, improvements in current zoning practice include the following:

The Role of the Board
and Related Qualifications of Members

The role of the board in zoning is frequently defined by a recital of the exercise of its powers. This is not an adequate criterion for judgment as to desirable qualifications for members. The more fundamental question is this: Is the function of the board to defend the public interest, as defined in the terms of the zoning ordinance by the legislative body, or to defend private interest, as expressed by applicants or appellants appearing before them? On this, an address by the late Chief Justice Maltbie of the Connecticut Court of Errors and Appeals is a classic and still-valid guide. In summing up cardinal principals, he stated:

> They are entrusted with the exercise of one aspect of the far-reaching police power of the state. They must always bear in mind that the issue before them is never primarily the profit or loss to a particular individual, but the maintenance of such a system of zoning as will best serve the interests of the community as a whole. They have great powers, but those powers are circumscribed and confined within the limits of the law governing zoning.
>
> They do not have an unlimited discretion to decide the issues before them, for such a discretion would be contrary to the very basis of American democracy.
>
> Finally, any zoning official who permits himself to be swayed by favor or prejudice, who yields to influence, political or otherwise, who arrives at a decision otherwise than in conformity to the governing rules of law and as a reasonable conclusion from the facts before him is false to the great trust imposed in him.[3]

"Maintenance of a system of zoning as will best serve *the interest of the community as a whole*" is the key phrase. Zoning imposes restrictions officially determined by the legislative body to be necessary to protection of that interest. Relief from such restrictions should not be granted except to the extent and in the manner allowed by law, however board members may be moved by compassion in personal hardship cases or by sympathy with those who would profit more richly if rules were relaxed. The board is established to protect the ordinance and the broad public interest, and not as an adversary agency.

Given this role, and considering the quasi-judicial nature of board duties, desirable qualifications for board members begin to emerge. Members should be selected who are dedicated to the interest of the community as a whole and can act in an informed, impartial, and judicious manner. Beyond this generalization, much will depend on the duties assigned to the board under the ordinance.

The original New York City Board of Appeals required highly qualified architects, engineers, and construction experts because it dealt with a variety of construction codes as well as zoning. If the ordinance assigns to the board special exception actions dealing with planned developments, similar expertise among its members may be highly desirable. If planned developments are handled by rezoning, however, having architects, landscape architects, or engineers on the board may not have such high priority.

In some instances, boards have been composed of representatives of special business interest groups, on the assumption that their views will balance out to approximate the general public interest. This is rarely the case, and, where conflicts of interest limitations apply, such boards may be handicapped in reaching decisions.

Among the retired, there are often persons with appropriate attitudes, training, experience, and familiarity with the community. Attorneys knowledgeable in zoning law may make good board members (if they are not active in local zoning practice). The League of Women Voters may contribute constructively to membership.

In many places, a member of the planning commission also serves on the board to provide liaison.

Considerations as to expertise on the board itself may be affected by expertise available to it from elsewhere in the jurisdiction and arrangements for its use.

Specialization and Division of Responsibilities

With growth in population and increase in range of governmental services, many jurisdictions now reassign responsibilities once the exclusive province of the board and provide for mutual support effort on others. This makes the most of expertise in the entire governmental framework—boards need not work unaided where there are planning commissions, professional planning staffs, legal departments, traffic engineers, and health officers.

The board's two appellate functions (involving appeals on grounds of error in decisions or interpretations of the administrative officials and appeals for variances) cannot properly be delegated under Standard Act zoning. On both of these, the board should, of course, be helped in its work by the planning staff and commission, the legal department, and such other agencies or officials as may be appropriate in particular cases. *Decisions* on appeals remain the responsibility of the board.

The third function, not appellate, is to "hear and decide special exceptions to the terms of the ordinance upon which the board is required to pass." Nothing in the Standard Act dictates that the board *must be* required to pass on any special exceptions. It has been firmly established that it may *not* act on special exceptions *not* specified in the ordinance.

The chapter on "Historic Orientation" noted that the 1926 Standard Act provided for a zoning commission *to prepare original proposed ordinance provisions*, or allowed a planning commission, if it existed, to be appointed as the zoning commission. This zoning commission was an ad hoc single-purpose body. Once its job was done, there was no provision for its continuance. The board of adjustment (or appeals) was appointed as a separate entity after the ordinance was adopted. As a quasi-judicial body, its prime duty was—and remains—appellate. In an era in which planning commissions were not always appointed, the board was also charged with handling special exceptions. At present, it would generally be preferable to have the planning commission and/or the professional staff make the determinations where decisions hinge on complex technical findings.

The Special Exception Work Load and How It Grew

In early zoning, there was some tendency to oversimplify things by dividing control of allowable uses into two classes:

Uses permitted by right. In single-family residence districts, to take a simple example, single-family residences were permitted by right, given proper lot and yard dimensions, etc.

Uses permissible only by special exception. Here we tended to lump things which might or might not be all right in a single-family district depending on various factors. In one sample list, special exceptions were required for schools; places of worship; hospitals; expansions of existing cemeteries; care of foster children in homes having more than six but not more than eight; day nurseries; home occupations; private clubs; rehabilitation centers; extensions of docks or piers; dockage or moorage of houseboats for occupancy on the premises; "temporary amusement activities in connection with a place of worship, school, or publicly operated recreational or cultural facility"; country clubs; and use of mobile homes for temporary construction offices.

To the special exception list for districts with more intensive uses were added both major and minor items—airports, drive-in establishments, planned residential developments, access to clinics in commercial districts for emergency vehicles on private ways through portions of adjacent residential districts, industrial parks, funeral homes, amusement parks, game parlors (including billiard and pool halls and establishments containing four or more pinball machines or electronic games), establishment or expansion of colleges (other than business) and universities, the keeping of domestic fowl, shopping centers, and so on and on.

Since there was to be public notice and hearing and debate on such matters, we often put off deciding and stating in the ordinance the standards and conditions determining whether or not particular classes of uses would be appropriate. That could all be done in the course of the proceedings on individual cases. But it meant also that there would be a lot of individual cases for the board to handle, and a lot of trouble and delay for applicants.

When we dumped everything we couldn't make up our minds about into the special exception chute, we overloaded board machinery. In many places, the board is charged with special exception duties beneath, above, and sometimes beyond it, in addition to those it may properly handle.

The solution for overcrowded board agendas is to eliminate from the special exception category those things on which board action is not really necessary, or which can be handled more advantageously in other ways.

Sorting Things Out

Three steps are suggested in sorting things out:

1. Decide what the problem is, or whether there is one.

2. Consider the full range of resources for solution.

3. Select the simplest acceptable answer.

Selecting from the special exception conglomeration above, and moving from easier to more complicated situations and proposed solutions:

Drop it from the zoning ordinance?   Neither the PTA nor the Ladies' Aid Society is likely to apply for a special exception to hold a bazaar, carnival, or spaghetti feast. If a traveling carnival is imported, licensing and control should be handled other than in zoning.

As to "temporary amusement activities in connection with publicly operated recreational and cultural facilities," *if* publicly operated, there is a responsibility for supervision which surely stops somewhere short of the board. What about temporary amusement activities otherwise or elsewhere? Surely this type of activity should be regulated other than through the ponderous processes of special exception zoning, and research into local codes usually reveals that it is. Move it out of zoning.

Let the health code deal with the keeping of fowl, etc.

Make it a use by right?   Starting with the most restrictive districts, schools and places of worship are traditional in single-family neighborhoods. If an ordinance requires special exception in such districts, why? It should be possible to permit by right those meeting specified standards—minimum land area and access from major streets, minimum yards, amount and location of off-street parking, protection of adjacent property from potential adverse effects, and any other reasonable prescriptions or proscriptions which would be likely to result from board consideration after public hearing.

Permit such uses by right if they meet such requirements and limitations. Reserve the special exception procedure for proposed schools and places of worship which don't.

This same approach has merit on other uses often found as special exceptions. State minimum requirements applying generally for the particular use, and by right. Then, if there are special circumstances under which a form of that use might be allowable without meeting the general standards, provide a special exception procedure.

(As another note on general approach, some ordinances use a cumulative compendium on special exceptions, leaving the first stated—"As for R–1 and in addition"—and adding more as they proceed through the districts. Others may have a list applying regardless of district. Neither arrangement has much to recommend it. For some uses, at least, it might be better to vary the requirement for special exceptions and the minimum standards applying by districts. Thus, taking places of worship as an example, even if the special exception requirement remains in the most exclusive residential districts, minimum lot size might be reduced in less-restricted residential districts, and both lot size requirement and the requirement for special exception dropped in districts other than residential.)

Moving on to minutiae ripe for removal in many special exception lists, consider the foster children entry. Six foster children in a home in a single-family district apparently created no problem. Had the obviously ad hoc addition here read "more than six," there might have been apparent justification for the special exception approach (although under the policies of the welfare agency involved, even six was unusual). But to reach an outer limit of two more requires an application for special exception, public notice, public hearing, and the decision of the board. Can this marginal threat to peace and tranquility mandate so massive a defense of the neighborhood?

Why is it in there?   Answers to this question (to be found implicitly or explicitly in records relating to the adoption of the provision) frequently reveal use of the special exception as a quick solution to a particular and sometimes one-of-a-kind problem. The case of the foster children is such an instance. Another is emergency vehicular access to clinics in commercial districts through portions of residential districts. A clinic had such a problem. It is not likely to recur elsewhere, nor should the solution be encouraged elsewhere. But embedding this one-shot solution permanently in the special exception provisions may result in repetition of errors committed at the first clinic. A traffic-bound site will be selected because it *can* get emergency vehicle access through the residential district at the rear.

If no sound reason existed or remains to support a special exception provision, remove it—particularly if it offers opportunity for the re-application of an inept solution.

Material remaining in the special exception listing may then be further sorted along the lines indicated below, leaving as special exceptions primarily those matters having substantial and lasting impact on neighborhoods.

Special Permitting to Fit Regulatory Needs

As a refinement of earlier practice, a special permit system is now used to handle cases from simple to complex with simple to complex procedures and determinations. Requirements for particular uses are no longer left to be set on an ad hoc case-by-case basis, but are set in advance to the maximum extent reasonably possible. Where technical determinations are involved, they are made by technical personnel, rather than by a quasi-judicial board.

"Special," as applied to these classes of permits, indicates only that there is action beyond that required for routine permitting. If issued, the permits involved cover all the usual items, but add conditions and safeguards as appropriate to the particular case or class of cases.

Language establishing such a system is cited below, along lines to appear in a new and expanded edition of *Text of a Model Zoning Ordinance, with Commentary.*[4]

Article 23. Special Permits, Generally

Section 2300. *Intent, Generally.*

In addition to zoning procedures and requirements relating generally to issuance of building permits and certificates of occupancy, a special permit system is hereby established. It is intended that this system shall assure special examination, review, and findings by appropriate agents, agencies, or bodies in connection with proposed actions particularly specified in this ordinance.

Special permit procedures and requirements as set forth herein are intended to apply in relation to use, occupancy, location, construction, design, character, scale, manner of operation, or necessity for making complex or unusual determinations, and to assure consideration of the particular circumstances of each case and the establishment of such conditions and safeguards as are reasonably necessary for protection of the public interest generally, and of adjacent properties, the neighborhood, and the jurisdiction as a whole.

In establishing this special permit system, it is intended to increase efficiency and reduce time required for processing applications by relating administrative responsibilities and procedural requirements to the degree of complexity and potential impact of the matters being considered. (Emphasis supplied.)

Section 2301. *Classes of Special Permits; Agent, Agency, or Body Responsible for Each; Referrals; Requirements Concerning Hearings, Generally.*

Five classes of special permits are hereby established, ranging from those dealing with uses, occupancies, and activities of a temporary nature or likely to have small but potentially adverse effects on adjacent and nearby properties to those with substantial potentially adverse effects on neighborhoods and/or the entire jurisdiction.

Procedures, requirements, and determinations range accordingly from simple to complex, with formal public notice and hearing not required on temporary activities, determinations concerning relatively minor matters, or matter affecting limited areas, or technical determinations, but with required formal public notice and hearing where actions proposed in applications are likely to have substantial area-wide or jurisdiction-wide influence.

Classes of special permits, the agent, agency, or body responsible for each, and general provisions regarding procedures are as follows.

Class A Special Permits

These are handled entirely by the administrative official, without referrals and without public hearing.

Using the Atlanta requirements, Section 1321, *Child Care Nurseries*, quoted at page (_____) as an example, the basic requirements have been analyzed and properly stated. The "special" determination is simple. The official makes a field visit to find out whether the fence or hedge is needed, and if so whether it fits the option requirements, where it should go, and how far it should extend to provide the protection intended. (This doesn't really require public notice and hearing before the board.)

Class B Special Permits

In these cases, still relatively simple, the administrative official must make a referral and is bound by the technical recommendations in the response.

For example, take off-street parking facilities with 10 or more spaces. Ordinance requirements might be that, in any district, parking for 10 or more vehicles shall be by Class B permit only. Mandatory referral would be to the Traffic Engineering Department (or local equivalent) for review on layout, curb cuts, width of accessways, access and exit arrangements, drainage and snow removal provisions, and the like. Technical recommendations on these matters become mandatory conditions and safeguards in the permit issued.

Class C Special Permits

Central responsibility here is with the planning director. Class C special permits involve relatively complicated technical determinations. The director may make referrals for advice and may hold meetings to collect information, but no formal notice and hearing of the kind required for special exceptions is involved.

For example, take a major shopping center. The land is zoned for the purpose, but in addition to generally specified requirements and limitations, the ordinance requires a Class C special permit covering approval of the site plan, staging of construction, traffic design, required covenants, and the like. The planning director, after consultation on traffic design, public works requirements, legal issues, and other matters involved, is responsible for issuance of the permit with its special requirements and limitations.

Special Exceptions
The board retains its Standard Act responsibility "to hear and decide special exceptions to the terms of the ordinance upon which such board is required to pass under such ordinance." If other steps suggested are taken, "special exceptions on which the board is required to pass" will center on effects of proposed developments on neighborhoods. On applications for special exceptions, the board should make referrals to the planning director (department). The director makes other required or optional referrals. The board gives "full consideration" to reports and recommendations received, but is not bound by them in making its determinations. Formal public notice and hearing is required.

For example, the ordinance provides for places of worship with sites of at least 100,000 square feet, located on major streets, as permitted uses in the district. A special exception is required for such uses on smaller sites, or without such access, and indicates findings which must be made and kinds of limitations which may be established.

An application is received to permit religious services and offices in a large home on a 50,000-square-foot corner lot on a minor street near the edge of an R–1AA district. There is a possibility that later an adjoining lot may be purchased. Acquisition would raise lot area to that required for the use by right. Present membership of the group is small but growing.

Staff reports that the surrounding neighborhood is made up of similar homes on large lots. Traffic on adjacent streets is not presently congested. City plan proposals call for widening the next street over to major status. The plan and other information submitted by the applicant suggest problems with provision of required off-street parking as internal alterations increase seating capacity for a growing congregation.

The board takes it from there. If the exception is granted, conditions and safeguards might include a time limit for continuance with provision for review and extension, restrictions on character and timing of activities, and provision for additional off-street parking.

A Word on Elected Governing Bodies, Appeals, and Permits
The elected governing body should not become directly involved in either the appellate or the permitting process. Generally, zoning appeals procedures are set by state law. Appeal from a board decision is directly to

the courts, and not through the governing body. Even where special acts or home rule powers allow such detours, routing appeals from the board through the governing body tends to mix political expediency with merit in decisions on particular appeals. On regular and special zoning permits (including special exceptions), the same considerations apply.

The body which makes law may amend it, but should not intervene to alter its application in individual cases.

Major Use Permits

Some governing bodies will insist on entering the permit arena, particularly on major developments likely to affect the entire jurisdiction or important segments. Examples here are such things as massive CBD redevelopment, convention centers, planned developments for housing, shopping, industry or other special or mixed-use purposes, and airports.

In some jurisdictions, provision is made for major use permits regulating such proposals. To establish a level for entry, and in some cases a barrier against intervention in lesser affairs, there may be a provision that such permits are required when, and only when, there are proposals for developments of regional impact. The required DRI report becomes an important guide in appraising the proposal and setting conditions and safeguards in relation to the permit.

Given the nature and scale of the projects involved, exhibits and reports required in this class of actions are voluminous and complex. Governing bodies involved in processing permits are prone to use prerogatives which do not exist when they operate in an administratrive capacity, as they do here, rather than in their legislative role. In action on permits, such bodies tend to waive, warp, add to, or subtract from requirements they have themselves adopted in ordinances. This they may not properly do except by formal amendment.

More Alternatives to Special Exceptions or Major Use Permits

Two devices may be used individually or in complementary combinations to handle developments which might otherwise be given special exception or major use status.

Planned Development (PD). This is an approach with broad application, usually to large-scale projects to be planned and developed under unified control, in a single operation or a programmed series of operations. The property must be rezoned to PD status, which involves the governing body in its traditional legislative role. Ordinance provisions laying groundwork for this type of amendment establish general procedures and requirements guiding actions on applications for rezoning of individual tracts.[5]

From beginnings 30 or 40 years ago, PD zoning has expanded from its original coverage of housing developments (PD–H districts) to a broad range:

PD–SC: Shopping centers, neighborhood, commercial, regional.

PD–HC: Highway commercial (for groupings of compatible uses).

PD–OP: Office parks.

PD–MC: Medical centers.

PD–IP: Industrial parks.

PD–MU: Mixed use, covering combinations ranging to new towns.

Special Public Interest (SPI) districts. PD districts are established for control of large-scale development, wherever it may be allowed to happen, although they may be used also for developments on a moderate scale. SPI designation is usually centered on areas, large or small, including individual sites.

The main consideration in SPI zoning is reflected in its title; "special public interest." Intent statement in parts of the ordinance providing for the establishment of such districts are of prime importance. They must indicate *what* is of such special and substantial public interest as to justify the regulations imposed. "Special public interest," as expressed in such intent statements, may take a variety of forms—protection of principal views, maintenance of specified character, access to waterfronts or through long blocks in the CBD, preservation of steep lands to inhibit excessive erosion and run-off and maintain natural cover, or whatever may be stated as a defensible subject of particular public concern.[6]

SPI designation may be used as an overlay, to modify details of existing zoning: "This is C–2, General Commercial, provided however that within the boundaries further designated as SPI–13, surrounding the Alvin Prexley residence and museum, sign limitations and architectural controls shall be as follows." Here, in keeping with the Prexley tradition, garish sign displays and ostentatious architectural manifestations would be inhibited.

Or SPI controls may take the place of other designations and work well in combination with PD regulations. For example, in Huntsville, Alabama, single-family detached development has crept up the slopes of the mountains. In Phoenix, Arizona, the pattern has spread to the lower edges of the hills. In both cases, upland owners, with justification, claim some sort of development rights. Huntsville's single-family neighborhoods pressed for large single-family lots on the steep slopes and protection of their views of the unspoiled woodlands. Some Phoenix neighborhood groups hope for protection of the open character of the visual surroundings and preservation of the southwestern way of life. There was some indication here, too, that larger single-family lots might be the answer.

There is a solution which might serve without yielding to the current but diminishing consensus that the American Way of Life requires infinite extension of large-lot single-family urban sprawl. In Phoenix and Huntsville, and many other places, there is a demand for other forms of housing—for retirees who are not concerned about the journey to work and will not compound rush hour traffic getting there, and for younger families with characteristics not requiring (nor able to afford) three or four bedrooms and several acres of land.

The answer suggested was to establish SPI districts covering the areas involved and to require that *any* development be handled by planned development-housing (PD–H) rezoning.

Maintain the low density sought through large-lot, single-family controls. *But prohibit single-family detached residences.* Instead, *require* attached and multifamily housing, require that a high proportion of land area (90 percent plus) remain as natural open space, and severely limit the amount of land usable for roads. Minimize road width requirements and establish drainage regulations limiting erosion. Use height controls that make sense in terms of view protection and the nature of the terrain.[7]

In the Phoenix context, this would result in the preservation of the southwestern way of life, exemplified by cliff dwellings and pueblos. In Huntsville, it makes sense in terms of both housing needs and environmental objectives.

Notes

1. This was apparently all that the original language intended. In the Standard Act, Section 3, *Purposes in View*, begins, "Such regulation shall be made in accordance with a comprehensive plan." A footnote to the section in a pre-1926 version of the act reads: "A comprehensive plan: Sound zoning implies a comprehensive plan. The zoning should be applied to the whole municipality at once. Piecemeal zoning is dangerous, because it treats the same kind of property differently in the same community."

Edward M. Bassett sheds considerable light on the matter both by what he does and does not say in *Zoning—The Laws, Administration, and Court Decisions in the First Twenty Years* (New York: Russell Sage Foundation, 1936), (hereafter cited as Bassett's *Zoning*). At p. 9, Bassett notes that zoning pioneers urged "that the entire municipality be zoned." At p. 12, he presses for "the old-fashioned way of zoning an entire town, which is supported by the courts in all states," instead of strip zoning along roadsides only. At p. 48, he says, "Inasmuch as lands situated alike should be zoned alike, the zoning map ought to cover the whole of the political subdivision." He opposes piecemeal zoning, for portions of a jurisdiction only, stating at p. 91, "No method could be more hazardous than this. Lawsuits would be inevitable and a comprehensive and coordinated zoning plan would be less attainable each year."

At no place in the Standard Act or in Bassett's commentary is there any definition of "comprehensive plan" or any discussion indicating that the term then had what is now its "traditional" meaning. The "tradition" developed in practice and in the courts and is now apparently binding so far as relation between zoning and the plan is concerned.

As Robert M. Anderson observes in *American Law of Zoning* (Rochester, N.Y.: Lawyers Cooperative Publishing Co., 1976), vol. 1, pp. 232–3: Notes clearly indicate that "the draftsmen intended to require some planning as an integral part of the zoning process. It is equally clear that no provision for the preparation or adoption of a written plan beyond the text of the zoning ordinance was spelled out in the act or referred to in the notes. It remained for the courts to give dimension to the requirement that zoning regulations be made in accordance with a comprehensive plan."

2. See, for example, Bassett's *Zoning,* p. 166.

3. W. M. Maltbie, *The Legal Background of Zoning,* an address to the Planning and Zoning Clinic, Hotel Bond, Hartford, Conn., Nov. 12, 1947.

4. Frederick H. Bair, Jr., and Ernest R. Bartley, *Text of a Model Zoning Ordinance, With Commentary,* 3rd ed. (Chicago: American Society of Planning Officials, 1966).

5. For such general language and detail on planned residential development, see Frederick H. Bair, Jr., "Intensity Zoning: Regulating Townhouses, Apartments, and Planned Developments," Planning Advisory Service Report 314 (Chicago: American Society of Planning Officials, 1974).

6. For general ordinance language and illustrative SPI applications, see Frederick H. Bair, Jr., "Special Public Interest Districts: A Multipurpose Zoning Device," Planning Advisory Service Report 287 (Chicago: American Society of Planning Officials, 1973).

7. Frederick H. Bair, Jr., "Height Regulation in Residential Districts," Planning Advisory Service Report 237 (Chicago: American Society of Planning Officials, 1968).

Appendix A
Play Fair in
Public Hearings
R. Marlin Smith
Partner, Ross & Hardies, Chicago

Consider the following excerpt from the proceedings of the planning board of the mythical city of San Cibola (as heard at a mock commission hearing at an APA conference):

Litigate: "Mr. Chairman, I would like to ask Mr. Hysteric a few questions about his testimony."

Wawfull: "Sorry, but we don't allow that."

Litigate: "I think I have a right to cross-examine to show that there is absolutely no basis for his inflammatory statements."

Wawfull: "We don't allow cross-examination."

Litigate: "Then you don't allow due process either."

"More legalese," grumbles the typical plan commissioner or zoning board member. "What is 'due process'? What's due and when? And why does it matter anyway?"

It matters because decisions about land-use regulation affect the rights of those who own and occupy property, and those rights enjoy the protection of the federal and state constitutions—including the Fifth Amendment to the U.S. Constitution, which states that no one may be "deprived of life, liberty, or property without due process of law."

The due process requirement has two aspects: procedural and substantive. Procedurally, the process by which a decision is reached must be fair to everyone concerned. Substantively, a law, rule, or decision must not be arbitrary; that is, there must be a rational relationship between the exercise of legislative authority and the achievement of some legitimate public purpose.

Nine points sum up the requirement for procedural fairness.

- **Give adequate and timely notice.** State enabling acts and municipal zoning ordinances invariably contain requirements for notice of proposed legislative and administrative actions on zoning matters and the hearings at which they will be considered. Due process goes further, requiring that the notice must be adequate (informative and easily comprehensible) and timely (allowing sufficient preparation time for a hearing).

- **Let everyone be heard.** Central to the concept of procedural due process is the requirement that all those interested in a decision must have a chance to offer their views and give testimony, provide evidence, or make a statement. By failing to conduct an adequate public hearing, a commission or board runs the risk that the regulation it adopts or recommends will ultimately be held to be invalid.

- **Allow cross-examination.** If a hearing is regarded by state law as quasi judicial rather than legislative, then all parties must have the opportunity to question their opponents' witnesses. (A good rule of thumb for deciding whether a process is quasi judicial is that it is if it's the final decision of an appointed board or commission. At least six state supreme courts have said that rezoning decisions are quasi judicial.)

The courts have been reluctant to require cross-examination in purely legislative hearings, probably because, in theory at least, such hearings are meant to be informative, not adversarial. Recently, however, an Illinois court did require a zoning board of appeals to give an opportunity for cross-examination in a rezoning hearing.

- **Disclose all.** All interested parties must have an opportunity to hear or see all of the evidence considered by the decision-making body. Private communications with the decision makers deprive other parties of an opportunity to respond. Worse, they destroy the credibility of the hearing process as a fair opportunity for everyone to be heard. (Recent decisions in the state of Washington have said that a public hearing must not only be fair, it must appear to be fair, and, if it is not, then any action based on it is void.)

A common breach of the disclosure requirement is the practice of considering, at the hearing, staff reports that have not been made available to the public in advance.

- **Make findings of fact.** The specific facts that justify the decision (the findings) must be spelled out. They are an essential aspect of due process in administrative hearings and without them the decision may be null. Findings of fact are ordinarily not required where the decision is characterized as legislative—as it is in most actions that involve text amendments or rezonings. The exception, a result of the well-publicized *Fasano* case in Oregon, is a decision about rezoning a particular parcel of land. But, even when not required, specific findings of fact, and recommendations based on them, are desirable.

- **Avoid conflicts of interest.** The courts will not permit a decision to stand if it involves a local official with a financial or other personal interest in the outcome. The appearance-of-fairness doctrine developed by the Washington courts, mentioned above, has frequently been used in that state to invalidate decisions in which even the indirect interest of one of the decision makers deprived the decision of the appearance of fairness.

- **Decide quickly.** Even adequate notice, a fair public hearing, and absolute impartiality do not guarantee due process if a decision is not made promptly. All parties have a right to expect prompt decisions, and failure to provide them is itself a failure to provide fair procedures.

- **Keep records.** All proceedings must be recorded completely and accurately. That means a stenographic record of all testimony heard and all statements made, not simply skeletal minutes of the proceedings. (Tape recordings are a poor second choice of doubtful reliability.) Anything less deprives the courts of the opportunity to engage in a meaningful review if and when the dispute reaches the judicial system. No hearing can be considered fair if the matters taken into account by the decision-making body cannot be reconstructed when its decision is reviewed by others.

- **Set ground rules.** Participants cannot prepare themselves for a hearing if they do not know the ground rules that will govern the process. Thus, a copy of the rules must be available to anyone who appears before the body. And at the start of every hearing, a member of the board or commission should briefly recite the rules that will be followed during the proceedings. It is good practice to require that those who expect to present evidence supply in advance a list

of the witnesses they propose to call and a brief summary of the
testimony anticipated. Reports or studies prepared by witnesses
should be filed in advance, as should staff reports.

The objective of procedural due process, in short, is to guarantee that
the decision-making body has before it all pertinent information—
ensuring, as far as possible, that the decision-making process will be
open, fair, and thorough.

This material is based on an article in *Land Use Law: Issues for the Eighties* (Chicago:
American Planning Association Planners Press, 1981), pp. 171–87.

Appendix B
Administrative Forms

Form 1

Board of Adjustment
Motions on Findings

TO GRANT AN EXCEPTION

The Board finds:

1. That the granting of this request is not contrary to the general intent of the Zoning Code and the public interest, and the property rights of the adjoining owners are substantially preserved.

2. That the exception granted creates no new variances and does not increase existing variances.

For extension of nonconforming structure or premises

Additional finding:

3. All questions on form entitled "Extension of Structures or Premises Devoted to Nonconforming Uses" have been answered in the affirmative.

TO DENY AN EXCEPTION

The Board finds:

1. That the granting of this exception would be contrary to the general intent of the Zoning Code or the public interest, or would be detrimental to adjoining property owners' rights.

2. That the request granted would create a new variance or increase existing variances.

Source: City of Tucson Board of Adjustment Rules and Regulations, 1976; Appendix C.

Form 2

Board of Adjustment

Motions on Findings

TO GRANT A VARIANCE

The Board finds:

A.   That there are special circumstances applicable to the property which, if strictly en-
forced, will deprive such property of privileges enjoyed by other property of the same
classification in the same zoning district; and which were not self-imposed; and that
this variance will not be a grant of special privilege to applicant; [add if applicable]
and that conditions have been imposed to make these findings operative.

B.   That it is also found:
1.   That because of physical circumstances—such as,
[☐ size   ☐ shape   ☐ topography   ☐ other]
no reasonable use can be made of the property without this variance.
2.   It will have no adverse affect.
3.   Light or air will not be impaired to adjacent property.
4.   Congestion will not be substantially increased.
5.   Neighborhood property values will not be substantially impaired.
6.   The amount of the variance is the minimum needed to afford relief.

C.   That the following conditions have been imposed:

TO DENY A VARIANCE

The Board finds:

A.   That the granting of this variance would give special privileges to applicant not enjoyed by other property in the same classification and vicinity and zoning district.

B.   That the special circumstances or conditions are self-imposed or were created by
applicant.

C.   That it is also found:
1.   There are no similar variances nearby.
2.   The variance would have an adverse affect.
3.   The amount of the variance is substantial.
4.   Reasonable use can be made of the property without this variance.

Source: City of Tucson Board of Adjustment Rules and Regulations, 1976; Appendix C.

Form 3

Board of Adjustment
Motions on Findings
Appeal from Zoning Administrator's Decision

TO APPROVE DECISION

The Board finds:

   1.   The Zoning Administrator's decision is proper.

   2.   His decision was based on following points:

        a. _____

        b. _____

   3.   These points should be upheld.

TO REVERSE A DECISION

The Board finds:

   1.   The Zoning Administrator's decision is improper.

   2.   His decision was based on following points:

        a. _____

        b. _____

   3.   Points ( )   ( )   should be overruled.

   4.   His decision should have been controlled by the following points:

Source: City of Tucson Board of Adjustment Rules and Regulations, 1976; Appendix C.

Bibliography

Many states publish manuals, guides, or booklets especially for zoning boards. These manuals generally discuss special state statutory requirements. Zoning board members or staff should obtain such materials for study. In addition, some local government planning agencies also publish guides that typically are distributed to new board members.

The following sources may be helpful to board members who want to learn more about zoning *in general*. To the best of the author's knowledge, this book is the only nationally published book devoted exclusively to the subject of the zoning board.

Babcock, Richard F. *Glass Houses and the Law: And Other Land Use Fables.* Colorado Springs, Colorado: Shepards, Inc., 1977.

------. *The Zoning Game.* Madison: University of Wisconsin Press, 1966.

------. "Zoning," Chapter 15 in So, Frank S.; *The Practice of Local Government Planning.* Washington, D.C.: The International City Management Association, 1979.

Bair, Jr., Frederick H.; Curtis, Virginia, ed. *Planning Cities.* Chicago: American Planning Association Planners Press, 1970.

Berger, Marjorie S. *Dennis O'Harrow: Plan Talk and Plain Talk.* Chicago: American Planning Association Planners Press, 1981.

Smith, Herbert H. *The Citizen's Guide to Planning.* Chicago: American Planning Association Planners Press, 1979.

------. *The Citizen's Guide to Zoning.* Chicago: American Planning Association Planners Press, 1983.

Thurow, Charles. "Zoning and Development Permit Systems," Chapter 4 in Getzels, Judith, and Thurow, Charles. *Rural and Small Town Planning.* Chicago: American Planning Association Planners Press, 1979.

Weaver, Clifford L., and Babcock, Richard F. *City Zoning.* Chicago: American Planning Association Planners Press, 1979.